THE DANGEROUS LIFE AND IDEAS OF DIOGENES THE CYNIC

Jean-Manuel Roubineau

Translated by Malcolm DeBevoise

Edited by Phillip Mitsis

OXFORD
UNIVERSITY PRESS

Oxford University Press is a department of the University of Oxford. It furthers
the University's objective of excellence in research, scholarship, and education
by publishing worldwide. Oxford is a registered trade mark of Oxford University
Press in the UK and certain other countries.

Published in the United States of America by Oxford University Press
198 Madison Avenue, New York, NY 10016, United States of America.

© Oxford University Press 2023

Originally published as *Diogène: l'antisocial*
by © PRESSES UNIVERSITAIRES DE FRANCE / HUMENSIS, 2020

CIP data is on file at the Library of Congress
ISBN 978-0-19-766635-7

DOI: 10.1093/oso/9780197666357.001.0001

Printed by Sheridan Books, Inc., United States of America

CONTENTS

FOREWORD

Ancient Greek philosophers tended to put their arguments and beliefs into practice much more earnestly and directly than those who take up the mantle of philosophy these days (usually academic professors)—so much so, in fact, that scholars speak of philosophy in Greek antiquity as a way of life. This way of contrasting old and new is extremely broad-brushed, of course, but one immediately thinks of Socrates incessantly buttonholing his fellow Athenians, challenging their most cherished convictions, and exhorting them to examine their lives since "an unexamined life is not worth living." By the same token, Plato portrays his teacher as preferring execution to a life in which he would be forced to give up his very public and evidently annoying methods of doing philosophy. Yet, although Socrates is often taken to be the preeminent example of a philosopher living and ultimately dying for his philosophy, arguably none of the ancient Greek philosophers lived in accordance with their beliefs in such an unremitting and all-consuming fashion as Diogenes the Cynic. It is reported that Diogenes chided Socrates for indulging in the luxury of wearing sandals, for socializing with the rich and famous, and for keeping a modest amount of inherited family property along with household slaves. Socrates, moreover, spent much of his adult life serving in Athens's imperialistic wars, the justice of which he did not question; indeed, he seems to have displayed a

certain degree of patriotic zeal. At the end of his life he disingenu-
ously avowed conventional religious belief and then cheerfully tried
to justify his acceptance of a verdict handed down by a jury of his
fellow citizens that condemned him to death for his philosophical
practices. In drinking hemlock he obeyed their decision, despite
being convinced that they were the ones committing injustice, not
he. None of this would pass muster with Diogenes.

Plato, for his part, dismissed Diogenes as a "Socrates gone mad,"
and it would appear that, even if unfair, this charge nonetheless
captures something of the extreme, intransigent, and flamboyantly
brazen character of Diogenes's life and thought. Diogenes, on the
other hand, considered himself to be eminently sane and virtuous,
and thought Plato little more than a Socrates gone soft—an elite,
aristocratic windbag with airy-fairy theories and a hypocritical life-
style to match. Both of these are polemical exaggerations, of course,
but whether we view a life such as the one Diogenes led merely as a
form of madness or as embodying harsh but necessary truths, we all
at some point, consciously or not, must come to terms with our own
societies' demands and with making our own choices in the face
of the kinds of dilemmas Diogenes's example presents. Should we
speak up, even if it is dangerous? Should we lead a life of social con-
formity even if its demands are psychologically debilitating or have
cruel and immoral effects on the lives of others? Do we too often
let economic worries and anxieties about social position and status
slowly drain our lives of meaning? Do we enjoy exercising power
over others, especially in our sexual relationships? These are just a
few of the questions that Diogenes's life and thought confront us
with in thinking about our own lives—questions that are posed in a
particularly thought-provoking and often outrageous manner in the
surviving reports of Diogenes's words and deeds.

Jean-Manuel Roubineau's *Diogène: L'antisocial* is in the grand tradition of French public philosophy. In bringing it before an English-
speaking audience, Oxford University Press has enlisted the services
of Malcolm DeBevoise, a prize-winning translator whose deep

background in ancient philosophy enables him to navigate the famous difficulties in moving between two capriciously different philosophical vocabularies and styles of argument (a word for which, as many Anglo-American philosophers like to point out, there is no straightforward equivalent term in French). Taking to heart the old adage that between England and France the best thing is the English Channel, many publishers just throw up their hands when faced with the prospect of translating French philosophical works.

Be that as it may, I think readers may be reassured that they will soon find Roubineau speaking to them in beguilingly familiar tones, with a certain amount of patented French wit and harmless irony, of course, but also with a refreshing candor about the actual state of our ancient sources. The narrative he pieces together about Diogenes's extraordinary life, as he readily acknowledges, can at best have only a general historical plausibility, but readers are given clearly marked starting points for further exploration. The incidents of Diogenes's career, like the stories attached to other lives that have taken on mythical status, have an emblematic value of their own. Moreover, the themes that Roubineau has chosen to emphasize have served as touchstones for a long line of subsequent thinkers who at times have adopted, at least in their writings, something approaching the intensity and vehemence of Diogenes's positions in attempting to draw aside the curtain dividing our social lives from our innermost natures. Freud and Nietzsche, for instance, both saw Diogenes as a man dedicated to living a thoroughly honest life, someone whose defiance of societal conventions amply illustrates the economies of repression that, for better or worse, support the complex structures of modern civilization.

Diogenes's life offers an especially rich and often amusing perspective on the social mores of his time, all the more since he himself was acquainted with a broad range of social positions, from his early years as the son of a wealthy provincial banker to the later experience of exile and slavery, finally becoming a public figure, playwright, and pedagogue. Roubineau deftly places Diogenes's travels and personal encounters in the context of the wider Mediterranean world of the fourth century BCE, laying special emphasis on his contrarian ideas concerning commerce and wealth, and his conception of the body as a tool for philosophy. The ways that Diogenes put his economic thought into practice, and his scandalous views of sexuality, in particular, have been a source of inspiration for a great many remarkably inventive defamers, partisans, imitators, and analysts through the centuries.

To find one's way through all the underbrush requires a sober and judicious guide. Roubineau is that and more. He argues that Cynic sexuality was actually rather conventional in certain respects, and, to a modern sensibility, retrograde. He often pauses to take a closer look at the purple passages, as it were, of the Cynic tradition, sometimes debunking traditional sources while taking care to clarify the textual evidence and giving reasons for his own judgments. His book ends appropriately by considering the various ancient accounts of Diogenes's death and their distinctive symbolic resonances. Diogenes wished for himself the kind of death that would have been thought horrific for a Homeric or tragic figure—to be left unburied, without the healing balm of communal rituals, and so never to be properly inscribed in collective memory. As Roubineau notes, antiquity's dangerous dog may have been successful in his first aim, but his place in collective memory is now secure, as scores of paintings and statues attest; his likeness is even to be found on the face of coins issued in the very place from which he had long before been exiled, allegedly for the crime of altering the coinage.

Perhaps Diogenes's most important philosophical influence was on the founders of Stoicism. As Stoicism developed and expanded its following, some aspects of this influence were often viewed with embarrassment, especially among later Stoics. Considering Stoicism's unsuspected resurgence in today's pop culture marketplace, it may be worth pointing out that the teachings of Zeno, Cleanthes, and Chrysippus, the school's original triumvirate, have precious little in common with the vulgar forms of

Stoic doctrine now being hawked from all corners of the internet and dispensed at weekend retreats for Wall Street and Silicon Valley warriors who come together to enjoy manly companionship fortified by selective readings from Epictetus and Marcus Aurelius. In order to get to the heart of Stoicism, one must first come to grips with Diogenes, the source of the early Stoics' most potent and provocative doctrines. The rigors of a self-sufficient life lived in accordance with nature—its poverty, disregard of public opinion, and impudent candor—are usually soft-pedaled in popular accounts of Stoicism today. Looking back to Diogenes, we are reminded of what initially made Stoicism so striking, inflammatory, and intellectually powerful.

A common view in antiquity was that Stoicism was "written on the tail of the dog," and it is this Cynic inheritance that gave Stoicism its bite; Stoicism, for its part, provided Cynicism with a more acceptable public face as well as a theological aspect, rooted in the idea of a beneficent Providence. Many scholars have seen the more philosophically palatable elements that Stoics share with Diogenes to have anticipated Kant's insistence on individual autonomy and will, unflinching moral rectitude in the face of life's choices, and a doctrine of divine mercy. In his unpublished lectures on logic, Kant parsed the question "What is a human being?" into three further ones: "What can I know?," "What should I do?," and "What may I hope?" For the Kantian, this final question ultimately leads to an inquiry into the nature of religion, but Diogenes, unlike the Stoics, who affirmed the operation of divine providence, found theological questions essentially unanswerable and in any case irrelevant to his primary task, which was to determine how one should live in accordance with nature and achieve a life of freedom and self-sufficiency. He showed a similar reticence about claims to knowledge. Diogenes's life offers us instead a series of exemplary moments demonstrating in a visceral way what it actually means to act in the light of an implacable commitment to freedom, rationality, and independence—this in a world driven by greed, lust, and ambition and governed by the social structures that foster these impulses. He would not have been much impressed by two hundred years of academic argumentation in defense of Kantian rationality and autonomy, bolstered by appeal to particular theological and epistemological doctrines.

Many commentators, of course, have found it easy to dismiss Diogenes either as naive and immature or as a blustering show-off craving attention. A disparaging view of philosophers more generally is no doubt coeval with the origins of philosophy itself. Certainly such a view continues to flourish today, especially whenever a professor resorts to abstractions to illuminate the practical problems of life. In the case of Diogenes, to be sure, we are presented with a particularly stark example of ethical obstinacy, since in answering the question of what we should do, his every action seems to have been calculated to call into question even the most mundane of our ordinary pursuits—pursuits that shield and distract us from values that it is easy to give lip service to as we go on living lives he would have regarded as proofs of cowardly self-deception. Parallels with the great Abrahamic religions abound here, of course, except that Diogenes thinks there is no divinity to help or hinder us morally, no original flaw in our nature that can keep us from realizing our true happiness, and certainly no future celestial rewards or punishments to spur us into action now. It is unlikely, of course, that any of the readers of this book will immediately cast away their possessions, say what they think with no restraint, and live in the streets with the carefree self-sufficiency of their dogs. But as Roubineau weaves his narrative, reviewing the many episodes in Diogenes's life that cannot help but stimulate further reflection, it is hard sometimes not to feel rather more sheepish than blithely dog-like.

Roubineau gives a good idea of the range of Continental scholarship on Diogenes and the Cynics, but there are two indispensable sources in English that have more extensive Anglo-American bibliographies: *Diogenes the Cynic: Sayings and Anecdotes, with Other Popular Moralists*, trans. Robin Hard (Oxford: Oxford University Press, 2012), and *Lives of the Eminent Philosophers: Diogenes*

Laertius, trans. Pamela Mensch (New York: Oxford University Press, 2018). For an account of Diogenes's world, see Duane W. Roller, *Empire of the Black Sea: The Rise and Fall of the Mithridatic World* (New York: Oxford University Press, 2020).

Phillip Mitsis
July 2022

ACKNOWLEDGMENTS

Many thanks to Olivier Coquard for having suggested that I write this short book and for generously commenting on a draft version.

My thanks, too, to Nathalie Bloch, a computer graphics specialist at the Université Libre de Bruxelles, for having created the map of Diogenes's world, and to Fabrice Delrieux for his insight into the numismatics of Sinope.

Finally, thanks to the staffs of Éditions Frémeaux & Associés and Presses Universitaires de France for their assistance, and in particular to my editors, Claude Colombini and Paul Garapon.

Jean-Manuel Roubineau

I would like to thank Drs. Margherita Bolla and Alberto Cavarzere for obtaining the necessary permissions to include the photograph of the Verona stele, and Alessandro Barchiesi for his intercessions. Special thanks to Stefan Vranka, Executive Editor at Oxford University Press, for conceiving the project and seeing it through to a successful conclusion, and also to Ris Harp, Kimberly Walker, and the rest of the OUP production team for making the process both efficient and agreeable.

Phillip Mitsis

MAP

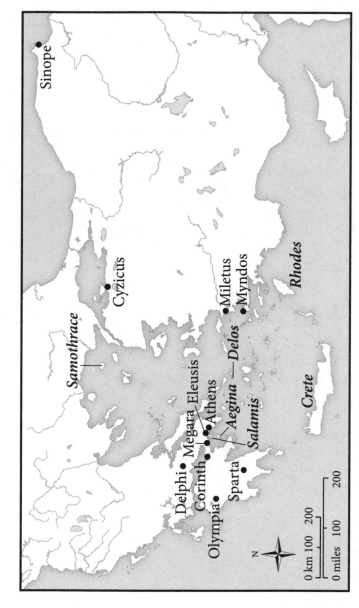

Cities and Islands of the Greek Aegean World That Diogenes Is Supposed to Have Visited. © *Nathalie Bloch/CreA-Patrimoine/Université Libre de Bruxelles*

Introduction

Even bronze is aged by time, but not all the ages, Diogenes, will
destroy your fame, since you alone showed mortals the rule of self-
sufficiency and the easiest path through life.

Inscribed on the base of the bronze statue erected by the city of
Sinope in honor of Diogenes, shortly after his death, these lines were
composed by one of his disciples, Philiscus of Aegina.[1] His poem,
while it insists on the philosopher's renown in the Greek world of
his time, also makes a bold prediction: Diogenes will not be forgotten! More than two millennia later, time has taken it upon itself
to confirm the justice of this forecast. Diogenes's memory has in fact
not been extinguished. In 2006, the modern Turkish city of Sinop
erected a new statue (Fig. 1), proclaiming itself, by this gesture, the
birthplace of the founder of Cynic philosophy. Diogenes is shown
standing on a barrel, holding a lamp, a dog at his side. On the bulge
of the barrel there is a second representation of the philosopher,
here shown curled up with a book. Still more recently, Greece has
issued several commemorative coins bearing the image of Diogenes
(Fig. 2), who is shown naked, leaning on a staff, with a dog on one
side and, on the other, the large ceramic jar he called home for a part
of his life.[2]

Exiled from the city of his birth, an outcast, mocked and insulted
by his contemporaries, Diogenes has become a tourist attraction and

a patrimonial figure, adaptable to any purpose, however unexpected. Almost fifty years ago, in 1975, his name was given to a medical condition: Diogenes syndrome, a behavioral disorder marked by withdrawal from society, poor personal hygiene, domestic uncleanliness, and excessive hoarding of objects of all kinds. And some fifteen years ago, in 2005, Diogenes having long been a symbol of frugality, his name was given to a European Union program aimed at reducing obesity, DIOGENES, an acronym for Diet, Obesity, and Genes.

But this very modern and persistent impulse carries on an older tradition. Diogenes has been a source of inspiration for Western artists since the Renaissance (Fig. 3). The highest honors came in the nineteenth century, in particular with two famous paintings by Jean-Léon Gérôme and John William Waterhouse (Figs. 4 and 5). The first shows Diogenes seated at the opening of his jar, adjusting his lamp under the gaze of four dogs. The second shows him once more seated in his jar, now holding a scroll, with a lamp set down nearby; three elegant young women look down upon him from an adjacent staircase. Some years earlier Honoré Daumier had devoted a series of caricatures to Diogenes, depicting him alone or in the company of the flamboyant Athenian statesman Alcibiades or Alexander the Great. The lithograph published in 1842 (Fig. 6), where Diogenes appears as a ragman, is accompanied by a brief poem composed by M. de Rambuteau:

> What, then, is Diogenes doing with a lamp?
> some foppish young men wondered out loud.
> I am looking for a man, he said, and with my slow lusterless eye
> I do not see one; this did sorely vex them.[3]

There are a number of reasons for Diogenes's abiding place in collective memory, beginning with his shockingly unconventional behavior, the best-known instance of which, incontestably, is his practice of masturbating in public. To this needs to be added his embrace of mendicancy[4] as a livelihood and his occasional habit of living in a large ceramic jar on the edge of the Agora in Athens. Two episodes in particular contributed to the formation of the legend surrounding him: on the one hand, his extraordinary encounter with Alexander the Great and, on the other, the disputed circumstances of his death. But, above all, Diogenes's notoriety is bound up with the role he played in formulating a Cynic philosophy and encouraging its propagation, from the fourth century BCE down through the Christian era. His legacy was considerable, not only in respect of the challenge he posed to established authority but also because of his indifference to material comforts and his commitment to a cosmopolitan conception of citizenship. Diogenes's teaching nourished a great many schools of thought, in antiquity and long afterward.

And yet in spite of his lasting influence on philosophical inquiry, Diogenes has remained the victim of two kinds of mistreatment, the first administered by the ancients, the second by the moderns.

A Misunderstanding

Since antiquity Cynicism has regularly been passed over in the annals of schools of philosophy and Diogenes himself dismissed as a harmless scatterbrain. In the first half of the second century BCE, Hippobotus, compiler of a list of philosophers and author of a treatise on philosophical sects, enumerated nine schools without mentioning Cynicism. Diogenes Laertius, whose biography of Diogenes, composed in the third century CE, is the only one to have come down to us, rightly objected to this omission, emphasizing that "Cynicism is also a school of philosophy, and not, as some say, merely a way of life."[5]

The misunderstanding arose in large part from the fact that Cynicism is more than a body of doctrine; it is a philosophy of action, of ideas put into effect by its adherents. It does not pretend to the status of a philosophical system. It has no grand intellectual ambitions. Its purpose is a purely practical one, animated by a desire to be immediately comprehensible to all people, educated or uneducated. The Cynic therefore cannot be a *scholar*, detached from what he speculates about; he must be an *agent*, the exemplar of his own convictions.

In addition to being reproached for a lack of theoretical sophistication, Diogenes and his followers were regularly accused of immorality. Cicero, though he approved of Diogenes's emphasis on free speech and independence of mind in relation to personal life, was by no means the first in a long line of critics who charged that the Cynic philosophy must be rejected in relation to social life, since its advocacy of shamelessness undermined moral sensibility and all that is "upright and honorable."[6]

In the eyes of the ancients, then, by denying the dignity and function of philosophy, Diogenes brought about his own downfall and that of Cynicism as well. The fact that in everyday language the term "cynicism" came to designate, not the school descended from Diogenes, but an attitude based on the rejection of hypocrisy and a mistrust of social conventions and received ideas, has done a disservice to the philosophical tradition of Cynicism by unjustly restricting the meaning and scope of its ideas.

The demotion of Cynicism in antiquity has been aggravated by its neglect by modern scholarship. When Diogenes has been seriously studied at all, it has been within the confines of a single field, the history of philosophy, and from a single point of view, which sees him as the founder of a philosophical tendency, nothing else. Very few economists, anthropologists, sociologists, or historians have regarded Diogenes as worthy of their interest. And yet philosophy is not the only thing he has to teach us. There is much more.

A Distorting Mirror

Many aspects of Diogenes's life cast light upon the Greek city-states of the fourth century BCE. His peregrinations give us some idea of the place reserved for foreigners in these urban centers, and of the mobility of populations in a Mediterranean world that was much more open and connected than in previous centuries. Moreover, contrary to the familiar idea of fixed hierarchies in ancient society, Diogenes's career testifies to the mutability of social status during this period, he himself having in the course of his life passed through every civic condition, successively citizen, resident foreigner, slave, and, finally, free man.

More generally, by his furious rejection of norms of all types, whether social, economic, or political, Diogenes illuminates their contours. Taken together, his transgressions amount to a negation of the standards of civic life. One thinks of his decision to live by begging, his refusal to marry, his celebration of a spontaneous sexuality, his contempt for property and his insistence on the paramount need for self-sufficiency, his scorn for privilege and wealth, his rejection of customary attachments, and his cosmopolitan outlook.

Diogenes delighted in bluntly pointing out the contradictions, the small-mindedness, in some cases the sheer absurdity of prevailing social conventions. And yet, unavoidably, he was a man of his own time, not always able to escape the hold of popular prejudice. Much more than he would have wished, Diogenes sometimes resembled the very people he scathingly criticized. In this respect, he interests us as much by what made him like them as by what made him different from them.

The portrait of Diogenes I present here is divided into four chapters. I begin by following Diogenes through the main stages of his life: citizen of Sinope, exile, resident foreigner in Athens and Corinth, slave following his capture by pirates, and his sale in Crete to a rich Corinthian who made him steward of his estate and tutor to his children, then released him. It was as a free man that he lived out the rest of his days.

In the second chapter I consider Diogenes's economic position, the social worlds he frequented, and the relation between his way of life as a mendicant philosopher and his thinking about wealth and poverty, freedom and slavery.

I go on, in the third chapter, to study the idea of the body that Diogenes proposed and incarnated, the Cynic ideals of simplicity and living in accordance with nature, and the appeal to animals as a model for human conduct in relation to diet, sex and marriage, and exercise and health.

I conclude by examining Diogenes's purposes as educator and founder of a school, his desire to transmit his philosophy, and his criticism of traditional philosophical schools (notably his quarrel with Plato), as well as the means he adopted to make his teachings known (foremost among them, speaking one's mind frankly and without fear of giving offense) and the risk of physical harm to which this policy exposed him. Finally, I take up the question of Diogenes's death and what the manner of one's death means for a philosopher.

Chapter 1

Diogenes, Foreigner

A little more than seven hundred texts document Diogenes's career, his philosophical positions, and the sayings attributed to him as well as the outstanding episodes of his life. For the most part these sources summarize and comment on Diogenes's writings and thought. Vanishingly little, by contrast, has come down to us from his own hand, notwithstanding that he was the author of a great many works, all of them lost but for a few fragments of a book of political philosophy, *The Republic* (in Greek, *Politeia*), transmitted by an Epicurean philosopher of the first century BCE, Philodemus of Gadara, in his treatise on the Stoics.

Which Sources, Which Diogenes?

One source occupies a preeminent place: Diogenes's portrait by a later Greek writer of the same name, a native of the Anatolian city of Laerte who lived in the third century CE. Diogenes Laertius set out to assemble a vast gallery of portraits of every philosopher of note from the birth of philosophy until his own time. His *Lives of the Eminent Philosophers* consists of ten books, the sixth of which is devoted to the Cynic philosophers, Diogenes foremost among them. Diogenes Laertius himself does not appear to have belonged to any philosophical school; he seems instead to have been rather more a poet who was interested in philosophy.[1] His approach, halfway between biography and doxography, alternates accounts of Diogenes's life with reports of his teaching. Diogenes Laertius's obsessive taste for anecdote rescued a great many moments of Diogenes's career, real or legendary, from oblivion.

Another important source of information about Diogenes takes the form of apothegms, short, pithy statements of the sort we now more commonly call aphorisms, conveying a striking insight or a piece of wisdom. These formulations were uttered (or were supposed to have been uttered) by Diogenes in the course of conversation with anonymous persons encountered by chance, or with disciples, or with statesmen and military figures such as Philip II, king of Macedon, his son Alexander, Craterus, Antipater, and Demosthenes.

Information about Diogenes in the form of apothegms has also been preserved in the Arabic papyri translated in the early 1990s by Dimitri Gutas.[2] Between the ninth and twelfth centuries, several Arabic collections of wisdom literature transmitted sayings of Diogenes drawn from prior collections dating to late antiquity. These prior collections have not come down to us, making the Arabic papyri all the more precious. Some of the apothegms found in the papyri are known, as it happens, in one or more Greek versions, making it possible to verify the attribution of these sayings to Diogenes. Other sayings have plainly been ascribed erroneously to Diogenes or else have been rewritten in a way that distorts the original anecdote. One finds, for example, a strongly Islamized Diogenes who urges the worship of a single God—"Diogenes in a djellaba," as one scholar has put it.[3]

In addition to this textual corpus there are figurative representations of Diogenes. But these images, whether they decorate a cameo, a mosaic, or a relief, depict a conventional and stereotypical Diogenes, and tell us less about the philosopher himself than about his posthumous notoriety.

Much of the surviving textual documentation concerning Diogenes was produced over the course of more than a millennium by members of competing schools of thought, with the result that he came to be endowed with a variety of virtues or vices as it suited the author's purpose. Some were favorable to Cynicism, such as the Stoic philosopher Epictetus and the emperor Julian; others were hostile to it, such as the Epicureans and certain Christian thinkers. Depending on the cause to be defended, Diogenes could be mythologized, idealized, and praised to the skies, or demonized, mocked, and reviled as the embodiment of every moral defect. The surviving documentation presents an additional difficulty, namely, that changing opinions within the Cynic movement itself produced differing accounts of Diogenes's life and thought, to the point that one sometimes has the impression of dealing with several Diogeneses.

An Uncertain Chronology

Diogenes lived to an old age, no doubt more than eighty years. The grammarian Censorinus, in his treatise on birthdays, *De Die Natali*, says that Diogenes died at the age of eighty-one. Diogenes Laertius, for his part, held that he lived to be about ninety. Several texts affirm that he died on the same date as Alexander the Great, which is to say during the night of June 10–11, 323 BCE. But this coincidence may be doubted; it is very probably part of the legend that subsequently grew up around Diogenes, as we will see. It seems likely he died sometime in the late 320s, perhaps in 323, a few days or weeks before or after Alexander, or perhaps in 324, if we can trust the report that he died on his way to the athletic competitions held at Olympia, and therefore during an Olympic year.

Regarding his birth, our sources are allusive, late, and contradictory. Only the *Suda*, a Byzantine lexicon of the tenth century based on medieval Christian compilations of ancient sources, gives a precise date. The article devoted to Diogenes says that he was born in the year when the Thirty Tyrants were overthrown in Athens, which is to say in 403. One of the versions of the *Chronicle* by Eusebius of Caesarea, initially composed in the early fourth century CE, asserts on the authority of an unidentified source that Diogenes was already a known figure in 396, but this would be impossible if he were then only seven years old, and scarcely less improbable even if his date of birth were to be put back by ten years or so, as is sometimes done.

Between his birth, sometime in the final years of the fifth century, and his death, in the late 320s, the chronology of Diogenes's life cannot be fixed with any precision. The few datable events known to us—three in all—took place during the years 338–336. According to Dionysius the Stoic, Diogenes was taken prisoner by Philip II of Macedon during the Battle of Chaeronea, in 338, and then promptly released. Two years later he attended the Olympic games and saw Dioxippus of Athens triumph in the pankration event (a competition combining the techniques of wrestling and boxing). And in late summer of this same year, 336, Diogenes met Alexander in Corinth.[4]

Citizen of Sinope

Diogenes was born in Sinope, a Greek city on the southern shore of the Black Sea, some 350 miles east of the Bosporus. Still today the archeological history of this area is rather understudied, unlike the Bulgarian, Romanian, Ukrainian, and Russian coasts, owing to the combined effect of the Cold War, on the one hand, which transformed the region into a buffer zone for several decades, and, on the other, the continuity of urban settlement from ancient times until the present day, which has made the earliest Greek remains almost impossible to locate.

Beginning in the seventh century BCE, an extensive network of Greek cities was established on the Black Sea. Sinope, founded in the second third of that century by colonists from the Ionian city of Miletus, on the eastern littoral of the Aegean Sea, was only one of many such settlements. Indeed, Miletus was so aggressive in this regard—Seneca counted seventy-five settlements, Pliny the Elder ninety—that the ancients spoke of the Euxine (the Greek name for the Black Sea) as a "Milesian lake."[5]

Between its founding in the seventh century (something that is known to us only through a treatise on geography due to Pseudo-Scymnus) and the fifth century, little is known of the history of Sinope. Only two things are certain. First, Sinope itself pursued an expansionist policy along the coastline of the Black Sea and was already recognized as a powerful city at the time of Diogenes's birth, possessing a large fleet and known for its willingness to intervene in regional conflicts. Second, the city underwent a period of political upheaval around the middle of the fifth century. It was ruled at that time by a tyrant named Timesileus, who may have been a vassal of the Persian king. Timesileus's overthrow by Athens in 437–436 led to democratic reforms. Athenian control over Sinope ended a few decades later, however; exactly when is unclear, perhaps in 411 or 405. Finding itself at a disadvantage in the Peloponnesian War, Athens was obliged to recall a contingent of soldiers that until then had been stationed in Sinope. The city's subsequent political regime is unknown to us.

The northern part of Asia Minor at this time was a theater for the ambitions of rival powers. Apart from competition among neighboring Greek cities on the Black Sea, notably Sinope and Sestus, a great many non-Greek peoples who occupied the interior of Anatolia (Paphlagonians, Cimmerians, Syrians, Assyrians, Leucosyrians, Hittites, Mariandynians, Chalybes, and so on) were subject to one degree or another to the authority of the Persian Empire, itself challenged by the Kingdom of Pontus and later, from the fourth century onward, the royal house of Macedonia. Forced cohabitation, whether peaceable or violent, with so many different peoples constituted one aspect of the geopolitical situation facing the Greek cities on the Black Sea. A second aspect was bound up with the geography and politics of the land immediately to the south: in addition to the natural obstacle of the Pontic mountain range, their freedom of movement was constrained by resistance from the Cappadocian and Paphlagonian kingdoms. Sinope adapted by turning to the sea, concentrating its economic activity on fishing and maritime trade for the most part, neglecting the hinterland that comprised its peninsula (known to the ancient Greeks as the Pedalion) and the narrow strip of land separating the city from the mountains (the Sinopitis). It was in this singular environment that Diogenes was brought into the world.

Banker's Son

Diogenes was the son of a citizen of Sinope named Hicesias. By virtue of his birth, then, he too was a citizen. Of his mother nothing is known. Hicesias, by contrast, is remembered for having held the office of *trapezitēs*. The term, attested since the fifth century, initially designated a moneychanger, someone who was authorized to exchange the foreign currency presented by traders and brokers for the local currency; his title came from the table or counter (*trapeza*) at which he conducted business in the agora.

The creation of this office was closely associated with the introduction of money and the growth in international commerce to which it gave rise in the sixth and fifth centuries. Greek cities appointed magistrates responsible for supervising both the minting of coins and market-based currency exchange. In Sinope, a public bank administered by Diogenes's father enjoyed a monopoly in this domain. Holding the office of *trapezitēs* was an index of family wealth and social status: since magistracies were unremunerated and their duties often time-consuming, they could be filled only by persons who had inherited a substantial fortune.

This evidence is corroborated by what may be inferred from our sources about Diogenes's education. We know that he learned to read and write; many anecdotes have come down to us in which he quotes epic and tragic verse. He was sufficiently familiar with athletic disciplines to be able to discourse on wrestling and to distinguish between beneficial and harmful forms of physical exercise. He had also been trained in the equestrian arts, which was to prove useful when he became tutor to the children of Xeniades in Corinth. This last detail is probably the clearest indication we have of Diogenes's privileged social background; the well-off were often referred to insultingly as *hippotrophoi* (horse breeders).

In most Greek cities, lessons were given by private teachers, hired and paid for by parents. Such an expense could be contemplated only by those who, in addition to having enough servants to spare their children the need to work, could afford the various kinds of instruction that a sound education required. These were people, in other words, who hoped that their children might aspire to a public career. Diogenes himself followed in his father's footsteps, holding the office of *epimelētēs*, a magistracy whose duties and powers varied widely from one city to another; in the case of Sinope, unfortunately, these are unknown.

Hicesias's name has been linked to coins circulating in Sinope bearing the stamp IKESIO, from the name of the public official responsible for monetary affairs. The minting of these coins, which dates to the last third of the fourth century, nonetheless cannot be attributed to Diogenes's father, who was already deceased by this time; the stamp seems to have been associated with someone of the same name, perhaps a member of the same family.

Images of Diogenes

Diogenes's portrait unmistakably appears on bronze coins current in Sinope during the Roman imperial period, which is to say long after his death. Only one example has come down to us. On the reverse one finds the letters CIF, standing for Colonia Julia Felix, the name adopted by Sinope after its conquest by Rome in 70 BCE. The coin must have been struck prior to the reign of Hadrian (117–138 CE), when the acronym CIF was replaced by CIFS, the last letter standing for Sino or Sinopes.

The obverse of the coin displays a bust of the philosopher, accompanied by the legend "DIOGENES." It is a conventional portrait—he is shown bareheaded with short hair, a long beard, and shoulders covered with a tunic—that testifies to the fame that Diogenes still continued to enjoy in Sinope at the beginning of the second century CE. The fact that he was a native son had led to the emergence of something like a cottage industry in memorializing flattery. Sinope was not an isolated case in this regard: Priene minted coins bearing the likeness of the sage Bias, Clazomenae of Anaxagoras, Ephesus of Heraclitus, Halicarnassus of Herodotus, Cos of Hippocrates, and Samos of Pythagoras.

The archetypal character of the numismatic portrait of Diogenes agrees with a good many other ancient representations of the Cynic. They are all of late date and stereotyped, including stone figurines modeled in the round, bronze and terracotta figurines, and decorative features imprinted on oil lamps; some are sculpted in relief, embedded in gemstones, or composed of painted ceramic tiles, as in the case of the portrait of Diogenes that appears in the Mosaic of the Seven Philosophers that adorns the floor of a Roman villa in Cologne (Fig. 7). Inserted in the bright orangish-red Cornelian gemstone conserved at the Thorvaldsen Museum in Copenhagen (Fig. 8) is an image of Diogenes seated at the front of his jar, leaning on a staff and conversing with a disciple who is facing him and holding a codex or a notebook. The philosopher is similarly depicted on an oil lamp fragment, emerging from the jar, his right hand raised in a gesture of explanation or welcome; above the image is the legend "DIOGENES" (Fig. 9).

The depiction of Diogenes on oil lamps, together with the existence of terracotta statuettes, objects of modest cost that were manufactured in large numbers, indicates that he was a familiar figure, not only to scholars, but also to people who lived in cities during the imperial period—proof of Diogenes's enduring place in the collective memory of both Greeks and Romans.

Various moments of Diogenes's life helped to sustain the legend that later grew up around him, few more lastingly than the debasement of the currency in Sinope, either by Diogenes or his father, a scandal that drove Diogenes into exile in Athens.

Counterfeiter

Much ink has been spilled over this episode since antiquity. The reports we have from ancient authors disagree with regard to the details of the affair. According to Diocles of Magnesia, Hicesias was guilty of restamping the coinage, forcing his son into exile.[6] According to the philosopher Eubulides, it was Diogenes himself who did this and who subsequently was obliged to leave the city with his father. According to anonymous sources cited by Diogenes Laertius, Diogenes was guilty of the fraud but his father, as superintendent of the public treasury, was arrested and died in prison; in the meantime, Diogenes managed to flee.[7]

The judgment of modern historians is divided. Some consider the episode to be authentic; for others it is merely one more detail of Diogenes's legend. What we need to do, I believe, is distinguish the nucleus of the episode, which is very probably true, from the apocryphal dross that has long obscured it.

The nucleus is this: Diogenes or his father, or perhaps both, counterfeited money in Sinope. Diogenes Laertius indicates that Diogenes himself, in his lost treatise *Pordalos*, acknowledged his guilt.[8] Hicesias's office as *trapezitēs* would have made the crime possible. In antiquity, forgers often plied their trade in specialized workshops; in some cases public officials supervised the activity of metalworkers. A treaty of the late fifth century between the cities of Mytilene and Phocaea provided for the issuance of a common currency; the text of the agreement explicitly contemplated the case where a magistrate responsible for regulating the money supply adulterated or otherwise debased the metal used for minting coins. Similarly, an inscription from the second century in the city of Dyme records an instance of counterfeiting in which a workshop plated coins made from an inferior metal with a thin layer of silver. Everyone involved, whether citizen or slave, was sentenced to death and executed.

Spurious coins were fabricated in several ways. In addition to the technique of plating, a similar result could be achieved by immersing a bronze core in a bath of liquid silver or gold, for example; or, in the case of coins consisting of a mixture of various metals, their true value might be substantially reduced by modifying the proportions of the alloy.

The inhabitants of Greek cities took great care to ensure that the coins circulating in their markets were genuine. They rubbed doubtful coins against the calcareous surface of a touchstone and then dipped the shavings in acid in order to gauge their precious-metal content. They tested a coin's authenticity by tapping it against the top of a marble (or possibly metal) table to be sure it rang true. They might also clip a coin in order to inspect its core, putting it back into circulation if nothing untoward was found. The very existence of such procedures suggests that the forger's trade was a flourishing one. It is hardly surprising or improbable, then, that Hicesias and his son should have been tempted to supplement their income by counterfeiting.

But this episode of Diogenes's life, no doubt true in its essentials, came to be embroidered in ancient tradition. Two legendary accretions are of particular interest. According to one account, Diogenes undertook to adulterate the currency following a visit to the oracle of Apollo at Delphi, or perhaps Delos. Misconstruing the meaning of the oracle's response, Diogenes concluded that the god was encouraging him to make counterfeit coins. The misunderstanding of an ambiguous answer, and the unfortunate consequences that flow from this, are a common-place of ancient Greek literature; one finds a great many examples from every period. In the case of Diogenes, the ambiguity and the misunderstanding arose from the polysemy of the Greek terms used by the oracle: *nomisma*, which might be taken to refer either to coinage, which is to say a monetary institution, or to social institutions in general—the laws, norms, and customs of a city; and *politikon*, which can refer to an individual city or to civic life generally. On hearing the oracle speak of *politikon nomisma*, Diogenes understood, wrongly, that he was being told to debase a local money supply, when in fact it was his destiny to undermine the conventions of urban life itself. This legend made it possible to minimize Diogenes's responsibility for the fraud, and may well have been devised for this purpose.

From this first interpolation a second one immediately followed, namely, that Diogenes's debasing of the currency prefigured his true vocation as a scourge of the established order. Intending the terms *nomisma* and *politikon* in the broadest sense, Apollo invited Diogenes to embrace his destiny; and in placing this anecdote at the very beginning of his biography, Diogenes Laertius made it the foundational moment of Diogenes's philosophical career. A comparable legend circulated in connection with Socrates, who, according to Plato, chose to become a philosopher as a result of dreams and after Chaerephon consulted the oracle at Delphi.[9] Zeno of Citium, the founder of Stoicism, is likewise said to have devoted himself to philosophy after consulting an oracle.[10] It may be that Diogenes took pleasure, after the fact, in giving the crime that led to his exile a philosophical and symbolic meaning. But the mythologized account is contradicted by the chronology of events: Diogenes himself says that his conversion to philosophy occurred in Athens, after he left Sinope, and therefore much later than the offense itself.[11]

Learning and financial probity are not always companions; a willingness to exploit the usual rules of economic behavior for the sake of financial gain is found in the biography of other philosophers. In the sixth century, Thales is known to have successfully speculated on the leasing of oil presses, having forecast an abundant olive harvest in Miletus and Chios on the basis of astrological observation.[12] In the next century, Gorgias managed never to pay taxes, by staying for only short periods of time in the cities where he gave lessons so that his name failed to be entered in the register of resident foreigners.[13] In the third century, Bion was sold into slavery as a result of a tax fraud committed by his father.[14]

It seems all but certain that Diogenes's crime, alone or in concert with his father, forced him to leave Sinope at once, before the municipal authorities had time to act. The date of his flight cannot be established with confidence, however. If one accepts that Diogenes attended Antisthenes's lectures in Athens, his arrival in Attica would have to be placed before Antisthenes's death in 366. In that case Diogenes must have come to Athens no later than the beginning of that decade. But it is possible that Diogenes only knew of Antisthenes's philosophy through his writings.

The Experience of Exile

Diogenes's exile was a decisive event, a moment of spiritual conversion. Plutarch tells us that exile and the loss of his possessions made Diogenes a philosopher.[15] Favorinus, an Academic Skeptic of the second century CE, went further, saying that Diogenes "became, from want, exile, and complete destitution, the most illustrious man not only of Sinope, but of the entire world."[16]

Exile, to the Cynic way of thinking, was the ultimate experience of detachment, renunciation, separation from everything one holds dear. It was altogether natural, then, that the lives of noble exiles should have been erected into models of exemplary behavior, Odysseus notably among them, of course, but also, and above all, Heracles, about whom Antisthenes and Diogenes composed several tragedies. Diogenes himself was regularly compared to Heracles. In an epigram mocking the Cynics of his age, the poet Antipater, in the second century BCE, praised an idealized Diogenes in the following terms:

> The wallet laments—and the fine sturdy Heraclean club of Diogenes of Sinope, and the double coat, foe of the cold clouds, fouled with encrusted filth, likewise lament because they are stained by contact with your shoulders. Diogenes was truly the dog of heaven; you are the dog that lies in the ashes. Cast off, cast off arms that are not yours. The work of lions is one thing, and that of bearded goats another.[17]

Similarly, the orator Dio Chrysostom, in the first century CE, imagined Diogenes paying tribute to Heracles, who placed liberty above all other things, showed no regard for social conventions, gave no thought to comfort, led a life of extreme poverty, submitted himself to trials of every kind, and chose death by fire. He was untroubled by heat or cold, had no need for bed, blankets, or floor covering. He severely punished bandits and scoundrels and lent a helping hand to honest people.[18] His condition, in other words, was one of permanent exile. This made him a tutelary figure for philosophers who, in allying themselves with his legend, recast the symbolic significance of exile by regarding attachment to the city of one's birth as a sort of imprisonment.[19]

In the Greek world of Diogenes's time, being uprooted from one's homeland was thought of as a tragic fate. Not being able to be buried in the same ground as one's forebears—to claim one's share of ancestral soil, as Euripides put it[20]—was a cause for intense suffering, a wound that could never be healed. A surviving fragment from a lost tragedy, in an evocative phrase, reminds the audience how sweet it is, after one's death, "to be hidden in the folds of the beloved land."[21] Diogenes set out to eradicate what he saw as a malignant sentimentalism.

Itinerant Philosopher

On leaving Sinope, Diogenes crossed the Aegean Sea and disembarked in Athens, a city that, in addition to welcoming exiles, was known more generally for the hospitality it showed to foreigners. As a center of learning, Athens had since the fifth century taken in many intellectuals, whether for shorter or longer stays, notably teachers of rhetoric and dialectic. Elite families throughout the Mediterranean sent their sons to Athens to receive higher education from teachers whose income depended largely on their patronage.

Diogenes Laertius mentions the presence, from the fifth century onward, of "young men from Pontus whom Socrates's fame had drawn to Athens."[22] Diogenes was not the only Greek from Pontus, nor even the first, to have settled in Athens. In the generations following, one finds several natives of Sinope among the Cynics, Diogenes's pupil Hegesias (known as "Dog-collar"), for example, and, a few decades later, Menippus. The inventory of foreigners resident in Athens—reconstructed for the most part on the basis of funerary stelae—confirms the presence of Sinopeans there from the fourth century up until the imperial period. Sinope itself belongs to a small group of cities from which we can identify more than a hundred people who left their homeland to settle in Athens during this time; for the fourth century alone, some twenty stelae commemorate Sinopeans who lived and died there. In spite of the distance separating Sinope from the cities of central Greece, the journey across Anatolia and the Aegean Sea evidently presented no great obstacle, as we know also from records of international athletic competition. A citizen of Sinope is known to have won the pankration event a few years before Diogenes's death at the games held near Oropos, a city lying some thirty miles to the north of Athens, during the festival of Amphiaraia.

We know that Diogenes resided in Athens for an extended period. Ancient texts report that he visited other cities, without giving a precise chronology of his travels. The list is a long one: Cyzicus, Miletus, and Myndos in Asia Minor; Eleusis, Salamis, Megara, Aegina, and Delphi in central Greece; Corinth, Sparta, and Olympia in the Peloponnese; Samothrace in northern Greece; and the islands of Rhodes and Crete in the southern Aegean. The motivation for these journeys, which gave rise to the familiar image of Diogenes as a wandering philosopher, is not known in every case, but it can be partially reconstructed.

Diogenes went at least once to Olympia, on the occasion of the games held there every four years. The most prestigious of the Panhellenic competitions, combining athletic and equestrian disciplines, it drew a sizable number of spectators from throughout the Mediterranean world. One detail I mentioned earlier makes it possible to date this voyage with confidence: Diogenes witnessed Dioxippus's victory in the pankration event, which we know occurred during the 111th Olympiad, and therefore in 336 BCE. Dioxippus triumphed *akoniti*, which is to say without having to compete, all of his opponents having withdrawn rather than face him. The names of two other Olympic champions whose performances Diogenes no doubt saw have come down to us as well: the runner Cleomantis of Cleitor, winner of the stadion race, and the boxer Mys of Taranto. Mys is remembered for having been crowned after fighting a series of grueling bouts; his victory was achieved with immense difficulty and only after absorbing a great many blows, with the result that he became a proverbial figure of self-sacrifice.

The games that year were memorable for another reason. Diogenes Laertius tells us that Diogenes took aim at Dioxippus in his hour of glory: "When a herald at the Olympic games announced, 'Dioxippus has defeated the other men,' Diogenes retorted, 'On the contrary! *He* defeats slaves, while *I* defeat men.'"[23] A few weeks later, witnessing Dioxippus's triumphal entry into Athens, Diogenes remarked on his fascination with the beauty of a young prostitute in the crowd of onlookers, and the weakness of soul that this betrayed.[24]

In criticizing Dioxippus, Diogenes attacked athletes in general and the whole system of values that sports upheld.

The usual reasons for going to Olympia were not thought to be respectable for a philosopher. In the fourth century, every Greek, child and adult alike, hoped to attend the Olympic games. In addition to the competitions themselves, which attracted the finest athletes in each discipline, there was the beauty of Olympia's sanctuaries and the dozens of statues that embellished them. Visitors were assured of witnessing memorable contests and marveling at the reckless speed of the chariot races. But Diogenes's admirer Dio Chrysostom refused to acknowledge that he might have gone to Olympia—and to Corinth, where the Isthmian games were held—for the simple pleasures that such spectacles offered, the thrilling sight of heroic triumph and tragic defeat. In the treatises Dio devoted to the Cynic, he emphasizes more than once that Diogenes did not have the same motives as the majority of those in attendance, "who wished to see the athletes and fill their stomachs, whereas he, I have no doubt, came to observe men and their folly."[25]

Dio furthermore reports that, in response to someone who asked whether he had gone there to watch the competitions, Diogenes said that he had gone not to watch, but to take part in them, to combat the many ills from which human beings suffer—anger, mistrust, sadness, desire, fear.[26] At the Isthmian games, Diogenes crowned himself victor, placing a wreath of pine on his head that the Corinthians sought to remove.[27] But beyond the interest in sporting events that Diogenes must have felt, no less than anyone else of his time, notwithstanding Dio's opinion to the contrary, his trip to Olympia may have been intended primarily to make his philosophy more widely known. The Olympic competitions were part of a religious festival held in honor of Zeus. Intellectuals since the fifth century had used such festivals as a forum for expounding their ideas. Herodotus, for instance, went to Olympia to deliver public lectures on the sidelines of the athletic events.[28] Before Diogenes, Antisthenes had welcomed the opportunity presented by these gatherings to disseminate his thought, and went to the Isthmian games for just this purpose.[29] Events sometimes took a more dramatic turn. The Cynic Peregrinus, to recall only the most stunning example, went down in history for having immolated himself on a funeral pyre in 165 CE during the Olympiad that year.[30]

Diogenes's voyage to Sparta seems to have been the result of intellectual curiosity, by contrast, and of a desire to study the social and political organization of this city at first hand. But despite his admiration for Sparta, he did not hesitate to practice his customary method of education through criticism. Aelian reports this pointed exchange between Diogenes and a citizen:

> A Spartiate cited with approval, in the presence of Diogenes, the verse of Hesiod "Nor would the ox die, if a neighbor were not evil." "But the Messenians and their oxen have died," said Diogenes, "and you are their neighbors."[31]

Similarly, Stobaeus reports that Diogenes, in response to an Athenian who observed that he had been careful not to take up residence among the Spartans, even though he sang their praises, said: "But even a physician, however great a healer he may be, is not going to live among sick people!"[32]

The reasons for Diogenes's other travels are harder to grasp. The list of cities he is supposed to have visited in Asia Minor, and particularly his presence in Miletus, renowned for the intense intellectual ferment of the sixth century there, may suggest that he made one or several journeys for philosophical reasons, the details of which escape us.

The Lure of Large Cities

Apart from these more or less prolonged excursions, Diogenes lived most of his life in two of the largest cities of the period, Athens and

Corinth. To walk from one to the other took only two days. Winters he spent in Athens, where the weather was mild, and summers in Corinth, cooled by the breezes traversing the Isthmus. He compared his mode of life to that of the Great King of Persia, who passed the winter in Babylon and Susa, among the hottest places in southwest Asia, and the summer at Ecbatana, where the climate was more agreeable at that time of year.

In Diogenes's time, Athens no longer enjoyed the economic vitality and political luster for which it was famous in the preceding century. Nevertheless it was still a dynamic and attractive city, with a population of several hundred thousand and supplied by the port of Piraeus, one of the busiest in the Aegean world. Corinth, for its part, was a commercial center that benefited from a most enviable geographical situation, an isthmus connecting central Greece and the Peloponnese by an overland route that passed between the Corinthian Gulf and the Saronic Gulf. Equipped with two ports, one on each body of water, and a portage road along which boats could be towed from one side of the isthmus to the other, the city, as a focal point of international trade and travel, profited from a flourishing economy.

From the philosopher's point of view, Athens and Corinth were ideal places for the propagation of ideas. According to Dio Chrysostom, Diogenes considered that "the sage should look to settle where fools are most numerous, in order to reprove them and correct their stupidity."[33] Here, or so it would appear, we encounter one of the oddest features of Diogenes's way of thinking: while rejecting almost all of the conventions of urban life, he did not avoid cities, as he might well have done; after all, like non-Greek peoples in the remote western and northern parts of the Balkan peninsula, not all Greeks lived in a municipal environment. But Diogenes did not have to avoid cities to be against them: he was *against everything in them*.[34] Most Cynic philosophers were deeply ambivalent about urban life. Antisthenes memorably compared the city to fire: come too close, you will get burned; but stay too far away, you will freeze.[35] A middle course needed somehow to be found: the Cynics' educational mission could be carried out, their apostolic role fulfilled, only in cities; and as a practical matter, mendicancy was feasible only in an urban setting. I shall come back to both these points.

In the cities of the Aegean world, then, Diogenes was in his element. Even so, he was not at home either in Athens or in Corinth. Having been born in Sinope, he was a citizen of neither one.

Resident Foreigner

In both Athens and Corinth, Diogenes enjoyed the relatively protected status of resident foreigner. This entitled him to fairly extensive judicial rights, comparable to those of citizens. He was subject to certain tax obligations, notably the payment of an annual assessment. The sum was not very great, roughly the equivalent of a week's wages, but its symbolic significance was considerable: non-payment entailed a loss of civil rights and immediate enslavement. Not that these rights amounted to much in the first place—resident foreigners could neither sit, nor deliberate, nor vote in the Assembly, nor could they hold any public office. Diogenes therefore cannot be described even as a "marginal citizen."[36] Like all resident foreigners, he was submitted to a form of sociopolitical relegation. As a verse from a lost tragedy bluntly put it, "Foreigner, you have not been born here, you will not subjugate our homeland!"[37]

We have seen that Diogenes did not always find himself in this situation during the course of his life. He started out as a citizen, in Sinope; then he became a resident foreigner, in Athens and Corinth; after that, a slave, in Crete and Corinth; and after finally being released by his Corinthian master, he lived out the days left to him as a free man. This experience may help us understand how Diogenes came to conceive of cosmopolitanism as an ideal.

The World as a City

Here we touch upon one of Diogenes's fundamental contributions to political philosophy. His invention of an early form of cosmopolitanism—and probably of the term itself—is well documented. Diogenes Laertius reports that when asked where he was from, he answered with a single word: *kosmopolitēs*—"I am a citizen of the world." Similarly, he maintained that "the only true commonwealth was that which was commensurate with the universe."[38] In the same vein, Lucian of Samosata, in the second century CE, quotes Diogenes as saying: "Let the whole world be bed large enough for me, let me call the universe my home."[39]

The cosmopolitan ideal lived on, having been adopted first by the Cynic school and then by the Stoic school. The following tragic verses are attributed to Diogenes's pupil Crates:

A single tower is not my homeland, nor a single roof,
But its citadel is the whole earth,
A home prepared wherein we may dwell.[40]

Likewise, according to Demetrius of Corinth, the world was to be seen as "the common home of all people."[41] But the continuity between ancient and modern cosmopolitanism must not be exaggerated: neither Diogenes nor his followers pleaded for a brotherhood of man. Diogenes himself, by emphasizing the contingent character of civic life and the principle of citizenship, seems to have been chiefly concerned with making people see the city-state not as a fact of nature, but as something artificial, a social institution.

Several aspects of Diogenes's career must have had a particular importance, none more than the fact that he spent the first part of his life in the city of Sinope on the Black Sea. His philosophical tastes and prejudices were crucially influenced by this early experience, even in connection with the simplest things of everyday life.

When he lived in Athens, for example, he continued to eat a small salted fish from the Euxine, known in local dialect as *saperdēs*, a kind of perch; he also fondly recalled the acidity of Pontic honey, which, like his philosophy, repelled those curious enough to taste it. More importantly, his formative years on the Black Sea brought him into contact with non-Greek peoples, which may have inclined him to elaborate a doctrine of cultural relativism. One finds this same familiarity with barbarous races in Antisthenes, whose mother was from Thrace.

Diogenes's experience of exile may also have played a role. Favorinus suggested that cosmopolitanism should be seen as a response to, and a consolation for, the loss of one's homeland.[42] Additionally, the condition of being a foreigner may have helped to weaken the appeal of naturalistic arguments, very commonly heard in the Athens of Diogenes's time, that based the entitlement of citizens to political power on the accident of native birth.

I now turn to the theoretical basis of Diogenes's philosophy, which, as we have seen, extended beyond the civic microcosm of particular cities to embrace the *kosmos* as a whole. For Diogenes devoted the main part of his philosophical career to undermining the foundations of urban life, beginning with a concerted attack on the system governing the accumulation and distribution of wealth.

Chapter 2

Rich as Diogenes

Diogenes the Cynic, on his arrival in Hades, after his wise old age was finished, laughed when he saw Croesus. Spreading his cloak on the ground near the king, who once drew great store of gold from the river, he said: "Now, too, I take up more room than you; for all I had I have brought with me, but you, Croesus, have nothing."[1]

Thus an anonymous poet imagined a face-to-face encounter in the hereafter between Diogenes and Croesus, celebrated king of Asia Minor, last of the Mermnades to have reigned over Lydia before the Persian conquest of 547 BCE. Croesus had drawn the better part of his immense fortune from the auriferous sands of the Pactolus River. A number of extravagant gestures contributed to his legend, among them his financing of the Temple of Artemis at Ephesus, one of the seven wonders of the ancient world, and the magnificent offerings made to Apollo at Delphi—three thousand head of cattle, many precious objects in gold and silver (beds, vases, jewels, statues), clothes dyed purple, a hundred bricks of pure gold.

In the eyes of the ancients, Croesus lastingly symbolized wealth, just as Socrates embodied wisdom and Milo of Croton manly strength. Diogenes, born more than a century after the Lydian king's death, never met him in real life. But had he been able to choose someone with whom to discuss the topic of wealth, he could not have hoped for a better partner in conversation. Above all, the content of this imaginary dialogue is consistent with what we know of the economic principles of Diogenes's philosophy.

Just as he mocked the impermanence of wealth, to which Croesus attached such great importance, Diogenes relentlessly denounced avarice as the dominant characteristic of the society of his time. Love of money, he said, was "the motherland of all vices."[2]

Diogenes was not content with developing a theoretical argument; he went on to work out its practical implications and then to act on them through a series of radical choices, notably the decision to live by begging. The whole of Diogenes's economic thinking is based on a conviction that may be summed up in three words: wealth is ridiculous. Money, material goods, patrimony—these things are merely lures, mirages, illusory ends in the pursuit of which men can only lose their way.

The Useful and the Useless

But wealth was not the only chimera needing to be combated. Power, glory, and the obsession with social status were scarcely less pernicious. In taking issue with the existing hierarchy of values, Diogenes began by distinguishing between two types of actions: those that are aimed at producing useful results and those that are aimed at achieving useless objectives.

The interpretation that the ancients gave to the meeting between Diogenes and Alexander was wholly of a piece with the philosopher's mistrust of all those who coveted or exercised power. The historical basis of this encounter, often revisited by modern artists—Pierre Puget's marble relief is a famous example (Fig. 10)—has often been doubted. Yet it is not at all impossible that their paths crossed, given the chronology of Alexander's campaigns.

On acceding to the throne of Macedonia in 336 BCE, Alexander hastened to calm restive allies in central and southern Greece, and at the Isthmus of Corinth he was proclaimed commander of the expedition against Persia. It is very probable on this occasion that Diogenes, staying in Corinth for the summer, met him. The various versions of their interview are agreed in portraying Diogenes as defiant of Alexander's authority, refusing to show him the respect to which he was accustomed. According to the account that Plutarch gives in his life of Alexander,[3] Diogenes declined to join the assembled statesmen and philosophers in coming out to greet the king; instead he remained in the Craneion, a cypress grove on the outskirts of Corinth with a gymnasium where he had made his home. Alexander went there with a few companions and, finding Diogenes lying in the sun, struck up a conversation that has since become legendary; I shall come back to it later. The insolence that Diogenes displayed on this occasion in the presence of royalty was not new. Two years earlier, having been taken prisoner by Alexander's father, Philip II, following the Battle of Chaeronea, Diogenes had spoken rudely to him. Amused by his impudence, Philip set him free.[4]

Demagogues, no less than athletes, were objects of Diogenes's scorn; the crowns they were awarded by the mob he called "pustules of fame."[5] More unexpectedly, he warned against the danger of desiring to improve one's station in life, whether in the case of a slave yearning to be freed or of a foreigner hoping to become a citizen. Observing an emancipated slave celebrating his freedom with a group of friends, Diogenes expressed surprise, saying in a voice loud enough for all to hear that the proclamation of emancipation did not make him free, it served only to recall his enslavement: for if a man who has been emancipated does not understand what is required in order to fully enjoy his liberty, he is not more free after his emancipation than before.[6]

Diogenes's capacity for detachment with regard to his own condition is perhaps most clearly seen in connection with his enslavement after being captured by pirates. Cleomenes, a student of Crates, himself a student of Diogenes, reports in his treatise *On Pedagogy* that Diogenes's students wanted to ransom him, but he told them they were fools: "Lions are not the slaves of those who feed them; it is the feeders, rather, who are the lions' slaves. For fear is the mark of a slave, and wild beasts make men fearful."[7]

Diogenes managed to profit from enslavement, in large part because social standing did not matter to him in the least. The expanded rights and obligations that people hoped to enjoy by climbing the social ladder were, to his way of thinking, nothing more than a snare and a delusion. A century later, the Cynic philosopher Teles of Megara carried ambition of this kind to its logical conclusion, moving absurdly and irresistibly from slavery to divinity:

> If [the slave] is a domestic, he longs to be freed: "If ever such a thing were to happen to me," he says, "I would have everything." No sooner does he gain his liberty than he dreams of having a slave of his own. Once he has bought one, he hastens to buy another. One swallow does not make a summer, as he says. Two slaves, then a plot of land, then Athenian citizenship, then military commands, a kingdom, and, finally, like Alexander, immortality: if such a thing were granted him, I believe he would aspire to become Zeus himself![8]

Nevertheless, of all the risible and useless obsessions of human life, none preoccupied Diogenes and the Cynics who came after him more than the desire to accumulate wealth—in respect not only of the ways in which it was obtained and distributed, but also of the place it occupied in the popular imagination.

Diogenes's Economic Doctrine

Diogenes's thinking about economic matters needs to be set in the context of the singular intellectual environment of the fourth century BCE, a period that brought forth what were called "economic treatises" (*logoi oikonomikoi*)—scholarly works that made economic

life in general, and domestic economy in particular, an object of inquiry and analysis. This was new.

A technical vocabulary had begun to develop in the late fifth century. First there appeared the noun *oikonomos*, formed by the con-
junction of *oikos*, meaning "household, home, family"—considered
as the basic unit of production and of life—and *nomos*, "rule." This
term, from which the late Middle English *yconomye* was to be derived, designated "one who administers his own property." It was
accompanied by the verb *oikonomeō*, meaning "to manage the affairs of a household." The two terms were very rarely used to begin
with; we count only four occurrences before the end of the century.
Two more related terms date from about the same time: *oikonomia*,
which gave us our word "economy," and the adjective *oikonomikos*,
referring to the qualities of a good manager. These four words
marked the emergence of economics as a separate domain, distinct
from religion and politics.

The first economic treatises followed in short order. All the
leaders of the major philosophical schools of the period claimed
to have written one: among the Socratics, Crito, Antisthenes,
and Xenophon; among the Platonists, Plato himself, as well as
Speusippus and Xenocrates; among the Aristotelians, Aristotle and
Theophrastus; among the Stoics, Sphaerus. All but two of these
treatises have been lost, one by Xenophon, the other by an anonymous member of the Aristotelian school known as Pseudo-Aristotle.

It was among the Socratics that the genre of *logos oikonomikos*
came into being. Works of this type treated everything having to
do with *oikonomia*, which is to say the proper management of the
household, taking into account investment expense, labor costs, and
profit. Antisthenes, Socrates's pupil and Diogenes's spiritual father,
seems to have been the author of the first such treatise, of which only
the title, *On Victory: An Economic Work*, is known to us. A few years
later Diogenes followed his example with a treatise called *On Wealth*.

Between the end of the fifth century and the end of the fourth
century the orientation of these treatises underwent a change.[9]

Whereas the earliest ones were concerned with formulating principles of sound management, which were to be applied for the purpose of protecting a family's patrimony, the treatises composed from the middle of the fourth century onward took on a more moralizing tone, asking whether wealth is a good thing, whether a person can be both rich and happy, and so forth. It is probably in this latter vein that Diogenes wrote his work. Since *On Wealth* has not survived, his economic thought can only be partially reconstructed on the basis of the apothegms that have been attributed to him. These are nonetheless enough to establish not only Diogenes's mastery of the subject, but also, and more generally, his interest in linking household management to larger questions of public administration.

Three anecdotes concerning the philosopher as economist are of particular interest. In the first, Diogenes admonished a young spendthrift who had run through the fortune left to him by his father and now found himself obliged to live on a diet of olives, bread, and water, saying to him: "If you had been intelligent enough to take your morning meal in this fashion, you would not be forced by necessity to make it your dinner."[10]

According to another, having been bought on a slave market in Crete and brought to Corinth, where his new master made Diogenes tutor to his children and steward of the household, the philosopher showed remarkable talent in discharging his responsibilities. According to Diogenes Laertius, he "performed all his duties in such a manner that Xeniades went about saying, 'A kindly deity has entered my house.'"[11]

From a third anecdote we learn that Diogenes likened civic administration to household management. To a man who had played music for him he said: "By men's minds are their cities and homes well-ordered, not by the twanging of lyres and the whistling of flutes."[12] Protecting a patrimony required the same qualities as the administration of a city's affairs; for Diogenes, they were comparable, if not actually identical activities. Both were the object of a new way of conceiving the tasks of management, which led to a corresponding devaluation of manual labor that took hold among elites of the fourth century and thereafter. It is hardly surprising that Diogenes, who preferred begging to working with his hands, should have found the idea congenial. In this he took his place in a larger philosophical movement, inaugurated by Socrates, aimed at redefining wealth and poverty.

Rich but Penniless

When Aristippus, another one of Socrates's pupils, who went on to found the Cyrenaic school, asked him what profit he took from philosophy, Diogenes replied: "The ability to be rich without having a single obol."[13] Conventional opinion was rather different, to say the least. Usually associated with patrimony, wealth was considered to be both a means and a proof of social success. Most people sought to preserve, and if possible to increase, the value of their estate with a view to transmitting it intact to their children. To claim that one could be rich while at the same time being penniless may seem an empty paradox, at best a piece of intellectual provocation. But there was something more to it than mere bluster. Socrates and Antisthenes had said the like of this before Diogenes, in the late fifth century and the early fourth century. Diogenes drew his inspiration from them. Xenophon, another heir to these traditions, spoke in very similar terms.

In Xenophon's *Oeconomicus*, composed in the 360s, the figure of Socrates, talking to a very wealthy Athenian named Critobulus, expressed pity for him. Noting Critobulus's amused surprise, Socrates explained that although his personal fortune was at least one hundred times smaller, he considered himself to be sufficiently rich, and Critobulus to be poor. He went on to say, "I have enough to satisfy my wants, but I don't think you would have enough to maintain your style of life and support your reputation, even if your fortune were three times what it is,"[14] alluding to the various financial obligations to which the wealthiest citizens were subject.

In the *Symposium*, Xenophon reports a comparable remark by Antisthenes, who says that he takes pride in his wealth even though he does not have an obol, and no more land than one would need to dust oneself with before wrestling.[15] Seen in this way, a poor man is not poor in any objective sense, merely someone whose needs are greater than his means.

Diogenes followed Socrates, Antisthenes, and Xenophon in distinguishing between the fact of poverty and the feeling of poverty, or, to borrow the vocabulary of Pierre Bourdieu, between *misère de condition* (actual poverty) and *misère de position* (perceived poverty).[16] Whereas the fact of being poor characterizes the condition of a person in the lowest economic class, the perception of being poor affects a person who is unable to support the financial obligations imposed by membership in a particular social class. From this point of view, Greek tyrants could be thought of as poor to the extent that they suffered from a chronic sense of dissatisfaction.

The distinction made by Diogenes and his predecessors between being poor and feeling poor resulted in part from the special place occupied by the rich in the cities of the period, particularly democratic cities. The wealthiest citizens and resident foreigners were required to assume public responsibilities, whether it was a matter of paying extraordinary taxes, bearing the cost of liturgies, or financing expenditures in the general interest (organizing banquets, maintaining warships, and so on).

This practice helped to make the concentration of wealth in the hands of a few socially acceptable and permitted the city to balance its accounts without having to levy taxes on the entire population. In the eyes of notables, however, sponsoring festivals, dressing elegantly, and supervising numerous slaves constituted a substantial expense, above and beyond the need to behave in a manner appropriate to one's social position. Teles recalls the case of Metrocles, a philosopher of the Peripatetic school who had known wealth and poverty in succession. When he was rich, he was permanently in want. But on becoming a Cynic and divesting himself of his inheritance, the problem disappeared:

> For until then he had to wear leather sandals and a cloak of fine wool, live in a grand house attended by young slaves and frequently entertain at dinner, taking care to see to it that there were ample quantities of fresh bread, choice meats, and sweet wine, a rather great extravagance.[17]

Poverty therefore had its advantages. The experience of being poor, Diogenes believed, compelled one to be a philosopher almost immediately, more quickly than even the most persuasive speech could do.

In the fourth century, the conception of wealth in terms of sufficiency, and therefore as a result of an equilibrium between needs and means, was something new, particularly in Athens. In the fifth century, rich Athenians had had no reason to be concerned with reducing their expenditures, for private extravagance was generally approved. But now the idea gained currency that the wealthy man had a duty to preserve his patrimony so that it would remain available in perpetuity for civic purposes. This had the effect of ratcheting up the pressure on the rich as a class. Public responsibilities that until then had fallen upon individuals were now borne by groups. In Athens, and other cities as well, where liturgies made it increasingly difficult to make ends meet, because it was no longer possible to find enough citizens to cover their costs on an individual basis, a regime of collective financing was instituted. In this context, Diogenes's reason for "call[ing] people who inherit great estates great paupers" is more easily understood.[18]

This idea is intimately bound up with a central concept of the new economic thinking: autarky. The term derives from the verb *arkeō*, meaning not only "to protect, to aid someone," but also "to be sufficient for, to be enough for." In ancient Greek, *autarkeia* denoted the situation of someone who succeeded in becoming self-sufficient, not in the modern sense of producing everything one needs, but in the sense of making up for what one lacks by means of that which one has an excess of.

From the confluence of the ideals of sufficiency (*autarkeia*) and frugality (*eutelia*) there arose among the Cynics the practice of mendicancy. The historical record does not allow us to determine with certainty whether Diogenes became a beggar before becoming a philosopher or whether he rejected the idea of working for a living as a matter of philosophical principle. Some authors have attributed responsibility for his decision to Antisthenes. Plutarch reports the following remark by Diogenes, an expression of gratitude disguised as a reproach: "In rags [Antisthenes] clothed me and condemned me to poverty and cast me out of my home."[19]

The possibility cannot be ruled out, however, that Diogenes had resorted to begging as a direct consequence of the poverty in which he found himself on fleeing Sinope, before resolving to devote his life to philosophy. However this may be, once he had become a philosopher, his mendicancy, whether or not it was prior to his conversion, came to be invested with a quite particular meaning.

The Choice of Mendicancy

The life of destitution Diogenes led is described by ancient authors on many occasions, and in great detail. His daily diet was meager: barley cake, water, olives, a small fried fish perhaps, a bowl of lentils (or fava beans on a good day), a few vegetables or roasted chestnuts, myrtle or cornel berries, apples, figs. As the proverbial Greek expression has it, Diogenes was impoverished to the point of licking a few grains of salt.[20]

Our information agrees with what is known of mendicants in Greek cities of the period. Yet Diogenes did not complain. Antiphilus

of Byzantium, a poet who flourished in the first century CE under
Nero, described his material circumstances in an epigram:

> The wallet and cloak and the barley-dough thickened with water,
> the staff planted before his feet, and the earthenware cup, are
> estimated by the wise Dog as sufficient for the needs of life.[21]

But the beggar's life cannot be reduced solely to its material aspects,
for constant insecurity was compounded by social degradation.
Mendicants were seen as violating a cardinal principle of Greek social life: *philia*. Often translated as "friendship," the term referred to
something much larger—the whole set of bonds of reciprocity that
individuals establish, not only within the framework of the family,
to begin with, but also in their relations with neighbors and, in the
broadest sense, the community made up by all the inhabitants of a
city. *Philia* was understood to constitute the main line of defense
against the hazards of life, a form of social security binding together
people who could thereby rely on one another in times of difficulty.
The entire social edifice of urban existence owed its robustness to
these many thousands of intertwined relations.

But mendicants were excluded from this virtuous circle of mutual aid. In the third century CE, Artemidorus of Daldis, in his book
on the interpretation of dreams, formulated an illuminating analogy.
To dream of giving alms to a mendicant, he said, foretells vulnera-
bility to the greatest injuries, even loss of life: "Beggars have this in
common with death, that alone of all people, like death, they take
something without giving anything in return."[22] They cannot benefit
from the mechanisms of solidarity that *philia* offers, not even within
their own family, whose goodwill they rapidly exhaust. Thus the proverbial saying that "not even a beggar's parents are his friends."[23]

To give oneself over to a life of begging was therefore synony-
mous not only with precariousness, but also with exclusion and
mistrust. The mendicant occupied the lowest stratum of society,
in certain respects lower even than the slave, who, by virtue of

belonging to a household, was protected by his master in proportion to the capital he represented and the affection he inspired. In this regard, mendicancy in a Greek city in the fourth century BCE was not comparable with the activity of the same name in a Christian city of medieval Europe, where a beggar was regarded as providing someone who gave him alms with an opportunity to work toward the salvation of his own soul. In a Christian context, then, mendicants were valued for rendering a spiritual service. Aelian, by contrast, described the consequences Diogenes faced for choosing a life of mendicancy: "Diogenes was bereft of all company and left all alone. He neither received anyone, because he was so poor, nor did other people invite him into their houses."[24]

The singular character of Diogenes's choice of livelihood, and that of his followers, proceeds from just this. He justified his choice by symbolically inverting the ideas usually associated with mendicancy, transforming its presumptively unilateral and parasitic nature into a reciprocal relation: in exchange for whatever donations he received, he dispensed advice and philosophical enlightenment. Xenophon, in a similar vein, quoted Antisthenes as saying: "I now begrudge no one but display my abundance to all my friends and share the wealth of my soul with whoever wants it."[25]

Diogenes took the view, then, that he did not beg, which would have been shameful; he asked, which was perfectly legitimate. In ancient Greek, these two actions are expressed by cognate verbs that are nonetheless semantically opposite: *aitein* (to beg) and *apaitein* (to ask for something to which one is entitled). In this way the requirement of reciprocity was made compatible with mendicancy.

The Jar and the Barrel

Homeless, needing a place to sleep that gave at least some protection against the elements, Diogenes took refuge in various places, depending on the city and the season, most famously in an earthenware storage jar located in the Metröon, a sanctuary of Cybele on the western side of the Agora in Athens. According to Diogenes Laertius, "He had sent word to someone to provide him with a little house, [but when] the man delayed, he took as his dwelling the [jar] in the Metröon."[26]

Diogenes's jar—often, wrongly, called a barrel—has become a cliché in the history of philosophy, like Montaigne's tower and Freud's couch. If Diogenes Laertius can be trusted, Diogenes was by no means alone in resorting to one as a means of shelter; the Cynics who came after him seem to have done the same thing. The sort of ceramic container (*pithos*) that Diogenes slept in was quite large: a man could stand up in many of them. They were usually used for storing foodstuffs—grains, oil, and wine—and often were anchored in the ground for the sake of stability and cooler temperatures. In spite of their uncleanliness and residual odors, and the fact that the very sizable circumference of their mouth offered little protection against the cold and rain, these jars would no doubt have been serviceable as temporary accommodations. The technical constraints of their manufacture and the amount of clay required made them relatively expensive. An inventory of the goods confiscated from persons who had desecrated statues of the god Hermes in Athens one night in the early summer of 415 BCE[27] lists *pithoi* valued at between thirty and fifty drachmae (whereas amphorae, small two-handled storage jars, cost only a few obols) and were counted as real estate, sold along with a house. It was certainly in a *pithos* of this sort that Diogenes chose to dwell for a time, even though we cannot say what its original use was.

In some of the Latin sources describing Diogenes's domestic arrangements he is said to have lived not in a jar, but in a barrel or cask, the Greek *pithos* being translated by the Latin *dolium*. The consequences of this semantic displacement were to be long-lasting: a good many of the modern representations of the philosopher show him inside or next to a barrel, including the statue erected in his honor in the Turkish city of Sinop in 2006. "Le Tonneau de Diogène," an illustrated story for children published in 1886

(Fig. 11), gives some idea of how deeply rooted this idea had become in the collective imagination by the late nineteenth century. It shows Diogenes being tormented by two scamps who have fun spraying him with water through a bunghole in the barrel, then rolling it over with him inside. But then they are hoist with their own petard: their clothes having gotten caught on nails sticking out from the barrel, they are carried along with it and end up being crushed under its weight.

In many countries of Western Europe in recent years Diogenes's imaginary cask has been exploited by the tourism industry, which invites visitors to stay in rental cabins in the shape of barrels equipped with comforts far above the Cynic standard (Fig. 12). The oldest literary trace of the transformation of jar into barrel is to be found in Seneca, in the first century CE, in a letter to Lucilius.[28] A few decades later, the satirist Juvenal likewise used the word *dolium* to refer to Diogenes's lodging as a barrel.[29] Juvenal was nonetheless aware that this object could not properly be called a cask, noting that it could not be burned (clay is much more fire-resistant than wood); but it could, by contrast, be cracked or broken, in which case Diogenes would have had to find another jar if he was unable to patch up the first one with lead.

The barrel became so much a part of the popular conception of Diogenes that it has sometimes interfered with scholarly rigor. The standard French translation of Diogenes Laertius, for example, justifies the decision to render *pithos* as "barrel" rather than "jar" on the ground that it would be undesirable to break with "the traditional image of Diogenes in his barrel."[30] One finds the same rendering in French versions of Julian's oration *To the Uneducated Cynics* and a sepulchral epigram dedicated to Diogenes and conserved in the *Palatine Anthology*.[31] We may nonetheless be sure that Diogenes cannot have lived in a barrel, for the like of it did not exist in the Greece of his time.

The invention of the barrel, a large flat-bottomed container made of curved wooden staves bound with metal hoops, is usually credited to the Gauls. The earliest texts mentioning barrels—Caesar's *Gallic War* and *Civil War*—date from the middle of the first century BCE, three centuries after Diogenes. The most ancient archeological traces date from the period associated with La Tène culture in its final phase, the first two-thirds of the first century BCE, and were found at Mortantambe (in Gaul) and Manching (on the Danube).[32] There were no barrels in Athens in Diogenes's time, then, only large ceramic jars.

Diogenes's resort to sleeping in one of these, in order to have a roof over his head, needs to be reexamined in the light of a particular historical moment, prior to his birth. At the outset of the Peloponnesian War, which between 431 and 404 opposed Athens and its allies to a coalition led by Sparta, the Athenian general Pericles recommended a bold strategy, avoiding battle with the Spartan infantry in favor of carrying on the war at sea. In the event he managed to persuade his fellow citizens to barricade the inhabitants of Attica behind the Long Walls, abandoning the hinterland to the enemy. The two walls, erected in the middle of the fifth century, connected the city of Athens to its port, Piraeus, to the southwest, guaranteeing access to the sea and therefore to supply lines. But the deterioration of sanitary conditions within the walls, which were separated from each other by a distance of about two hundred meters (650 feet), each one about seven kilometers (four miles) long, gave rise to an epidemic in 430 that soon decimated the population. A few years later Aristophanes mentioned the makeshift dwellings that had sprung up *intra muros*. By then, in 424, the war had been going on for seven years. Among these temporary accommodations were jars. The poet uses the term *pithaknē*, which refers to a small jar. He mentions also "vultures' nests" and "shacks"—all of them phrases that call to mind cramped and uncomfortable lodgings unsuited to prolonged residence.[33]

Like the term *pithos*, from which it is derived, *pithaknē* has been mistranslated in French. Aristophanes's translator in the Belles Lettres edition makes it a barrel. Similarly, in Bailly, the standard

Greek-French dictionary, the term is mistakenly rendered still today as a "small barrel."

Pericles's strategy of withdrawing behind the walls made improvised housing in an urban setting common, with the result that a form of lodging that formerly was rare or nonexistent now became a part of both the geographical and the mental landscape of Athenians. Until then, premature newborns who did not survive were virtually the only human beings relegated to such vessels, a practice known as enchytrism, in which the remains of children or animals were buried in a small vase. With the Peloponnesian War, jars took their place among temporary shelters in the city.

When Diogenes took to living in a jar a few decades later, on the edge of the Agora, he profited from the normalization of this practice. Accounts of the tragedy of the war had been passed down in Athenian families since the end of the fifth century, preserving the memory of the immense public health crisis created by Pericles's strategy and of the very difficult conditions of life to which a significant part of the surviving population had been reduced. By the middle of the fourth century, Diogenes's choice was no doubt much less incongruous than it would have been if he had been the first to live this way. Indeed, his decision seems to have been generally respected; when a reckless youngster broke Diogenes's jar, legend has it that the Assembly voted to provide him with another.

City of Clay

More generally, Diogenes's retreat to a *pithos* casts light on the preponderant place of the art of pottery in the daily life of the Greeks of his time. In Athens, the fourth century witnessed the flourishing of a particular form: the Attic red-figure vases with decorative motifs that were produced in the Cerameicus, the potters' district of the city, and adorned the homes of wealthy citizens. Ceramic work made its presence felt even in political affairs, where few people today would think of looking for it. In the fifth century, pottery shards (*ostraka*) were part and parcel of the procedure of ostracism—political exile voted by the Assembly—where each citizen wrote down on a vase fragment the name of the person he suspected of trying to subvert democracy.

The various episodes in which pottery figures in connection with Diogenes are revelatory. He threw away his drinking cup, for example, on realizing that it was unnecessary after seeing a child drink water by cupping his hands.[34] On another occasion, he used an earthenware pitcher in order to make a philosophical point: "When someone dropped a loaf of bread and was ashamed to pick it up, Diogenes admonished the man by tying a rope to the neck of a wine-jar and dragging it through the Ceramicus."[35] He also used analogies with pottery in order to make philosophical ideas more easily understood. John of Damascus reports him as saying:

> The education of children resembles the activity of potters: they impart to the clay the form and arrangement they desire, but they can no longer work it once it has been fired; in the same way, people who have not been educated at the cost of much effort during childhood cannot be transformed once they become adults.[36]

Whether it was a question of contesting the usefulness of pottery (the drinking cup), of using it for shelter (the ceramic jar), or of converting it into an instrument of philosophical instruction (the neck of the wine pitcher), Diogenes's world was made in no small part from clay; his use of a jar as a place to sleep and for protection against inclement weather is only the most striking manifestation of this. But the jar in the Metröon was not his only known residence in Athens.

Beggars' Haunts

Diogenes and his fellow mendicants found refuge where they could, in the interstitial spaces of the city, as it were—porticos and temple porches, accessible covered places in public view. Pointing toward the Pompeion, a temple near the city's main gate, the Dipylon, and the Stoa of Zeus, at the northwest corner of the Agora, Diogenes humorously remarked that the Athenians had constructed them in his honor, so that he could have a place to live.[37] The agora was also a place to practice philosophy. A passage in the *Vatican Gnomology* suggests that for him the agora was what a workplace was for a worker.[38] People came in large numbers to the adjacent sanctuaries, presenting an attractive opportunity for mendicancy. Sleeping inside the temples was prohibited, but beggars were able to sleep on their porches so long as they enjoyed the indulgence of magistrates and priests or otherwise were able to evade their attention. The Parthenon itself, architectural symbol of Athens's power in the fifth century and repository of the treasures of the goddess Athena, could have been used for this purpose. Teles imagined a dialogue between Diogenes and Poverty, who inquired of him:

> "Do I not give you lodging free of charge, the public baths during winter and summer, the temples?" Diogenes replied, "Can you offer me a more stately summer cottage than the Parthenon, this grand and airy place that I call home?"[39]

In addition to baths, forges were convenient places to visit in order to warm up. No doubt Diogenes investigated other possibilities as well, perhaps sleeping in empty tombs or abandoned houses. Lucian suggests as much. In *Philosophies for Sale*, Diogenes tells a prospective buyer that the life of a Cynic philosopher will require him to "leave the house of your fathers and make your home in a tomb or a deserted tower or even a jar."[40] The tower Lucian had in mind was probably either a farmhouse tower used for storage or a lookout tower. The tomb he mentions could have been a monumental mausoleum fallen into disuse, but while such structures were relatively numerous when Lucian was writing, they were still rare in

Diogenes's time. Diogenes himself would have been more likely to find refuge in tombs or walled courtyards.

Begging as a Way of Life

A life of impoverishment in the fourth century amounted to both a psychological and a physical ordeal. The common view of beggars likened them to parasites; whatever small assistance they received was furnished only very episodically by persons who feared that they themselves were in danger of becoming beggars. When Diogenes was asked why people sometimes showed charity to mendicants but not to philosophers, he lucidly replied, recalling the myth of Oedipus: "Because they assume they may someday be lame or blind, but never expect to take up philosophy."[41]

Nevertheless, the contrast Diogenes drew between the good fortune of ordinary beggars and the ill fortune of philosopher beggars is a bit forced. Whether or not they claimed to be philosophers, beggars were poorly regarded and mistreated in the cities of ancient Greece. Plutarch reports an anecdote that testifies to the fate that was habitually reserved for them. The scene unfolds in Sparta. In response to a mendicant who asked him for alms, a Laconian spoke bluntly: "If I should give you something, you will beg for more; and for the dishonorable life you lead he who first gave you something is responsible, for thus he made you lazy."[42]

Mendicants were thought of and treated as outcasts, people to be shunned. They were frequently reproached by ancient authors, who complained about their uselessness, comparing them not only to freeloaders who invite themselves to other people's parties without ever inviting them to parties of their own, but also to predatory insects and birds—hornets, scourges of the beehive, and wagtails, who lay their eggs in the nests of other birds. The rejection of requests for assistance was a part of daily life. When someone expressed surprise at finding Diogenes begging alms from a statue, he replied that he was trying to get used to being turned down.[43]

Such alms as there were chiefly involved food: bread or barley cake (*maza*), olives, a small cheese, a little salted fish. Monetary gifts were rare. But like many beggars, Diogenes took advantage of other opportunities. Offerings to the gods that were placed near altars were eagerly sought after; the difficulty was to escape the notice of the priests and remove the food before it spoiled. The altars of Hecate were the main targets of such larceny. Diogenes gladly resorted to this expedient, emphasizing that he saw nothing improper about stealing from a temple.[44] No doubt he also joined the crowd of scavengers who gathered in the agora to pick up whatever scraps of food vendors had left behind or were selling cheaply at the end of the day.

Diogenes was well used to living by his wits in cities. But traveling brought with it another kind of hazard that was less easily protected against—as, for example, when the ship taking him to Aegina was attacked by pirates.

Diogenes and the Pirates

Piracy was very common in antiquity. It was directed not only against ships, but also against coastal villages. People taken captive were sold as slaves everywhere in the Mediterranean or released on payment of ransom. Along with prisoners of war, victims of piracy constituted the principal source of supply for slave markets from the fourth century onward, though to a still greater degree in the Hellenistic period. The phenomenon is well documented by a series of inscriptions. Abductions by pirates and privateers are attested primarily in the Aegean Sea and the Black Sea, and secondarily around Sicily. Raids in the waters of Attica were especially frequent.

The pirates of the ship to which Diogenes was forcibly transferred were commanded by a captain who was sufficiently well known that his name has come down to us, though in different forms depending on the source: Cicero speaks of a Harpalus, Diogenes Laertius of a Scirpalus; the *Suda* calls him Skirtalus. In keeping with the practice of sailing a more or less great distance from the place where captives had been taken, Diogenes and his companions in misfortune were brought to Crete and sold into slavery there. This suggests that the pirates themselves may have been from Crete. Cretan piracy is attested from the beginning of the Archaic period; it is mentioned on several occasions in Homer's *Odyssey*, and recurs in documents dating to the second half of the fourth century.

By then it was so widespread that even Alexander the Great was obliged to take it into account in planning military strategy. When Alexander sent Amphoterus to deliver Crete from Persian and Spartan domination in the spring of 331, he ordered the admiral to begin by clearing Cretan waters of pirate fleets.[45] Considering Diogenes's advanced age when he was taken prisoner, it is reasonable to suppose that this took place sometime earlier that same decade, in the years after 340. What sets Diogenes apart in this case is not the fact that, having been born free, he was made a slave, for he was hardly alone in that, but the altogether singular attitude he adopted toward the condition of slavery.

Diogenes and Manes

Diogenes is said to have owned a slave named Manes. If this is true, we know from his name that he came from Phrygia; but we know next to nothing about his relationship with Diogenes. Phrygian slaves were numerous in Athens during the Classical period. Diogenes is unlikely to have bought Manes at the market there, however, having fled Sinope in poverty and resolved thereafter to devote himself to philosophy. It is far more probable that Manes belonged to the first part of his life, before his exile, and all the more because, by virtue of its geographical situation, lying to the northeast of Phrygia in Anatolia, Sinope was a natural destination for Phrygian slaves.

Be that as it may, we are told that Manes escaped. In the Greek world of the fourth century, this was a matter of the gravest concern; some masters went so far as to chain their slaves in closed quarters during the night. Various official measures were taken to reduce the risk of flight. Treaties were concluded between cities in Asia Minor—for example, the one between Miletus and Heraclea at Latmus, known to us from an inscription of the early second century BCE, which very carefully specifies the terms under which captured slaves fleeing Miletus for Heraclea and Heraclea for Miletus could be restored to their owners. Fugitive slaves had to be presented to the border patrol of the city where they were captured, then formally described in a letter addressed to the magistrates of the other city. The slave's master was then informed and, after paying an administrative fee, including the cost of feeding the prisoner, permitted to reclaim his property. For slaves taking refuge in sanctuaries, statutory provisions incorporated in the sacred laws vested powers of arbitration in the priests, as well as the final decision whether to return the slave to his master or to arrange for his resale to a third party.

As a private matter, masters severely punished runaway slaves when they managed to track them down. In addition to corporal punishment, our sources mention the practice of tattooing on the fugitive's forehead the instruction "Arrest me, I have run away"[46] or some similar phrase—thus ensuring that every slave bearing this legend would be the object of constant surveillance by the city's inhabitants.

Manes, although he was not apprehended, nonetheless met with a dire fate: while fleeing to Delphi, he was attacked and torn to pieces by a pack of wild dogs. Aelian, who recounts the episode, remarks that "[he] paid the penalty for his action in a manner appropriate to his master's name," alluding to the sobriquet given to Diogenes by his contemporaries.[47]

Diogenes's reaction to his slave's escape was one of indifference, the opposite of what would normally have been expected from a master. "It would be absurd," he said, "if Manes can live without Diogenes, but Diogenes can't live without Manes."[48] At the heart of Diogenes's lack of interest in owning a slave, manifest in a discourse Dio Chrysostom devoted to him entitled *Diogenes, or On Servants*,[49] is the Cynic conception of freedom and slavery: Diogenes, and those who followed him, sought to be the slave neither of any thing nor of any person, for whoever is unable to detach himself from his possessions and his desires becomes dependent on them. Accordingly, Diogenes called "slaves three times over" those who allowed themselves be ruled by gluttony, sex, and sleep.[50] No less than the other comforts and pleasures of existence, owning a slave could therefore be thought of, by a symbolic reversal, as a condition of servitude for his master.

Diogenes's understanding of slavery was enriched by the fact that, just as the seer Tireisias was reputed in mythological accounts to be successively man and woman, the Cynic had the leisure of observing the operation of the slave system from both points of view, having first been a master and then a slave himself.

Diogenes and Xeniades

Diogenes was sold on a Cretan slave market to Xeniades, a Corinthian passing through Crete. Diogenes Laertius indicates that he was a notable—wearing a robe with a fine purple border—and that he wished to entrust Diogenes with important responsibilities in his household.[51] It is possible that Diogenes's master was identical with a Corinthian of the same name mentioned by Sextus Empiricus, a Skeptic philosopher who lived during the imperial period. In *Against the Professors*, Sextus recalled that a Xeniades was described by Democritus (who died around 370 BCE) as having defended a number of philosophical positions, notably the view that "all things are false, all that which comes into being arises from non-being, and all that which perishes disappears into non-being."[52] If the two Xeniades were not the same man, the one might have been the grandfather of the other, in keeping with a well-attested Greek onomastic practice. But if they were in fact one and the same, it is unsurprising that Diogenes, finding himself sought after by a fellow philosopher, should have wished to be his slave.

Leaving to one side the testimony of Sextus Empiricus, the manuscript tradition has depicted Xeniades in an unfavorable light. Philo describes him as effeminate. The *Suda* says that he was a rich and dissolute Corinthian, which is to say someone who could be ordered about. Xeniades's treatment of Diogenes, in other words, particularly his permissiveness, was incompatible with virility, citizenship, and freedom.

The circumstances of Diogenes's sale, whether real or imagined, betray his unorthodox attitude toward the master-slave relationship. Noticing Xeniades among the crowd of bidders, he turned to the auctioneer and said, "Sell me to *him*; he needs a master."[53] This quip concealed a philosophical principle, founded on two key ideas of Cynic thought: on the one hand, that social status counts for nothing and that each person determines the boundaries of his own freedom; on the other, that servitude is only the power that one grants to others over oneself, or, more generally, the degree of dependence to which one willingly submits. As Julian put it, in his oration *To the Uneducated Cynics*: "That man is truly a slave over whom another man has power to compel him do whatever he orders."[54] It was therefore the slave's own behavior that made him who he was, regardless of the rights to which he was entitled by law.

After several years of service—agreeable, even rewarding ones from Diogenes's point of view, or so we are led to believe—he was freed by Xeniades. This should not come as a surprise. The practice of releasing slaves, no doubt as old as the slave law itself (dating to the sixth century BCE), was considered by masters to be a useful expedient, for two reasons. First, it made it possible to recover the capital investment in an aging slave by allowing him to buy his freedom. Second, if release was promised before actually being granted, it guaranteed the slave's willingness to carry out his assigned tasks for the duration of his service. While our sources are silent in the matter of Xeniades's motivations, these may have been less managerial in nature and more philosophical than in the majority of such cases.

On the basis of his personal experience of slavery, and as against the dominant naturalistic view—according to which a slave was a slave *by nature*, thereby justifying slavery as an institution—Diogenes argued in favor of treating people as equals, without regard for their position in urban society. To his mind, only the multiplicity of artificial needs that individuals create for themselves made some of them slaves. Just so, dependence was a matter not of social status, but of bodily needs and pleasures.

Chapter 3

Diogenes on the Proper Use of the Body

One day, or so it is said, he had arranged with a courtesan to come see him; as she was late, he rid himself of his sperm by rubbing his genitals with his hand, and after that, the courtesan having arrived in the meantime, he sent her away, saying that his hand had anticipated the nuptial song.

Thus Galen of Pergamum, the famous physician of the second century CE, described Diogenes's recourse to masturbation in one of his treatises.[1] Onanism, one of the sexual practices most frequently associated with Cynicism, contributed in no small measure to its perverse reputation. Diogenes in particular was known for engaging in it, shamelessly, for everyone to see. Diogenes Laertius reports that he masturbated in the marketplace, saying, "If only one could relieve hunger by rubbing one's belly."[2] He emphasized that it was Diogenes's habit to do everything in public, including "the acts associated with Demeter and Aphrodite."[3] Dio Chrysostom credits him with composing an apologia for masturbation.[4] Diogenes may have been inspired by the mythological example of Pan, god of shepherds, who was afflicted with great ugliness and an immoderate sexual appetite; lover of nymphs and young boys, often shunned, he did not hesitate to satisfy his sexual needs himself.

If Cynicism has rightly been described as a kind of *ascēsis*, which is to say a training of the body, plainly it was not based on a refusal of pleasure. In the earliest phase of the movement this tendency was less clear. Antisthenes would have preferred that pleasure be excluded from the Cynic way of life, holding that "pain is a good thing" and saying that he would "rather go mad than feel pleasure."[5] But Diogenes, who conceived of pleasure as a legitimate desire bound up with the body's elementary needs, while rejecting all forms of mortification, was to prevail.

Nature and Frugality

Modern interpreters of Cynicism fall into two rival camps. For some, the Cynics were fundamentally concerned to live life in accordance with nature (*physis*); for others, they were animated above all by an ideal of frugality (*euteleia*). Neither one of these principles by itself captures Cynic thought in its entirety; indeed, to reduce it to a plea on behalf of a return to nature amounts to overlooking the many social conventions of which they approved. The originality of Cynic philosophy arises instead from the way in which it combined the two principles. Depending on the case, human beings were thought to be able to achieve liberty and self-sufficiency, while avoiding servitude in its various forms, either by imitating the animal world or by simplifying their behavior.

Cynic philosophy is based on the idea that human beings have lost their way, having strayed from a primordial state of equilibrium. On this view, the world of living beings is divided into three strata and three species, each of which exhibits a characteristic degree of autarky. At the bottom of the scale is mankind. In the middle, the animal kingdom, admirably obedient to the logic of self-sufficiency and necessity, by virtue of which it occupies a position morally superior to that of mankind. At the top, the gods, who are wholly self-sufficient since they have no needs. This tripartite system is sometimes supplemented by a fourth stratum, populated by sages, below gods but above animals. In this connection, Diogenes says that "it was characteristic of the gods to need nothing, and of godlike men to need very little."[6] Men, being incapable of truly imitating the gods or of attaining wisdom, were therefore well advised to imitate animals.

The Animal Model

According to Philodemus of Gadara, Diogenes in his *Republic* urged people to live as dogs do. What did he mean by this? The most probable explanation is that the Cynics sought to do away with the traditional distinction between men and animals, and in this way to abolish the self-imposed limitations and prohibitions that disfigured human existence.[7] Animals provided men with an example that enabled them to learn to distinguish between natural (and therefore desirable) behaviors and behaviors that were the result of social (and therefore useless or harmful) customs.

Here again the Cynics dissented from orthodoxy. Earlier Greek conceptions of the human condition proceeded from a fundamental difference between men and animals, on the one hand, and men and gods, on the other. The myth of Prometheus is the first account we have of the origins of this distinction. With the keeping of meat for men, rather than the gods, their place was securely established midway between the divine and the animal.

In order to recast the symbolic implications of this myth, Diogenes and his followers sought to associate men with animals by rejecting not only funerary rituals, for example, but also various taboos, whether alimentary (such as cannibalism) or sexual (such as incest). The Cynics' adversaries missed no opportunity to rail against what they wrongly took to be an attempt to justify abhorrent practices. For the Cynics, it was a matter simply of taking the idea of life in accordance with nature to its logical conclusion. Diogenes himself used the example of cocks, dogs, and asses to discredit the prohibition of incest:

[Oedipus] knew that he had consorted with his own mother and that he had children by her; and subsequently, when perhaps he should have concealed this or made it legal in Thebes, in the first place he let everyone know the fact and then became greatly [agitated], lifted up his voice and complained that he was father and brother at once of the same children, and husband and son of the same woman. But domestic fowls do not object to such relationships, nor dogs, nor any ass, nor do the Persians, although they pass for the aristocracy of Asia![8]

In animals Diogenes found traits that he felt were worthy of imitation. Animals manifested their superiority in many ways. They were less anxious than human beings, untroubled by scruples, healthier, able to run faster, even to fly. But animals were not a model to be imitated in every respect. They were also capable of reprehensible behavior; the ant's propensity for plunder and robbery and the june bug's gluttony were proverbial.

Animals of various species were invoked, from the largest to the smallest, including fish, more reasonable than humans with regard to Aphrodite's pleasures; migratory birds and deer; also hares and other creatures who take the seasons into account. Mice, in their wisdom, were a source of inspiration. If Theophrastus is to be believed, Diogenes learned how to cope with the problems of daily life "from watching a mouse running about, not seeking a shelter or avoiding the dark or searching for any of the things that are generally thought desirable."[9]

Of all the animals in the Cynic catalogue, however, none occupied a more exalted position than the dog.

Diogenes and Dogs

In his own lifetime, Diogenes was called "the Dog" (*kyōn*) by his detractors. This disparaging nickname, source of the term "Cynic" (*kynikos*), was gladly adopted by the philosopher as a badge of honor. Diogenes's tomb, near the gate of Corinth, was adorned by a pillar on top of which stood a dog carved in Parian marble.[10] Yet his ambivalence about taking animals as a model for human behavior was unabated for all that. Diogenes was not prepared to identify himself with every kind of dog, and therefore insisted on making it clear what kind of dog he was. Several anecdotes are telling in this regard. The dialectician Polyxenes is said to have been indignant that people called him a dog. But Diogenes said to Polyxenes, "You too should call me 'Dog'; Diogenes is merely my nickname; I am indeed a dog, but one of noble breed who watches over his friends."[11] In a similar vein, Dio Chrysostom indicates that Diogenes compared himself to the dogs of Laconia: "Many people came to pat them and play with them at the marketplace, but nobody could quite bring himself to buy one, because they were not sure they could handle these animals."[12] He distinguished between different breeds and the traits peculiar to them: "Asked what kind of dog he was, he said: 'When hungry, a Maltese terrier; when fattened, a Molossian mastiff—breeds most people praise but wouldn't dare take along on a hunt, for fear of fatigue.'"[13]

Diogenes's likening of himself to a dog was selective in another respect. As he himself recognized, he often behaved in ways that no real dog would. Observing that "other dogs bite their enemies, whereas I bite my friends in order to save them,"[14] he discounted the gentleness dogs are well known for showing in the company of people known to them, and their aggressiveness toward strangers. In this regard he once more put himself at odds with Plato, his great adversary, for whom their benevolence toward friends and hostility toward strangers were essential qualities. In the *Republic*, Plato stresses that the human guardians of his ideal city should exhibit these same qualities, which are those of dogs with good breeding, whose "character is naturally to be able to be most friendly to those they are used to and recognize, but the opposite with those they don't know."[15]

As in the case of the Cynics, the name of the Stoic school likewise derived from a nickname. Zeno of Citium, its founder, taught under the covered portico of the Agora in Athens, known as the Painted

Porch (*stoa poikilē*); his pupils were called "those of the Porch" (*hoi apo tēs stoas*), whence the name "Stoics." But whereas this name came from a building and a place associated with the dissemination of Zeno's ideas, that of the Cynics arose from the manner in which their teaching was received and subsequently caricatured.

The fact that many explanations were given by the ancients for the nickname "Dog" no doubt contributed to its popularity and its persistence. The first of these is connected with the place where Antisthenes taught, a gymnasium within a sanctuary of Heracles situated in Cynosarges, outside the walls of Athens. Various etymological origins have been proposed for the name Cynosarges, among them "swift" or "shining dog" (*kyōn argos*) and "manifest" or "splendid dog" (*kyōn énargēs*). Antisthenes himself was the first to be nicknamed *haplokyōn*, a broad term that may mean "candid dog," "natural dog," or "dog with a simple cloak." The first sense is connected with Antisthenes's reputation for frankness, the second with the Cynics' desire to live in accordance with nature, and the third with the simplicity of their clothing.

The Cynics' behavior was dog-like in various respects. They practiced the art of *parrhēsia*, which is to say speaking freely, with the same honesty and candor that dogs display, being unable to conceal their emotions. They led a simple life and openly satisfied their natural urges, without shame. They were often dirty. They were content with scraps of food. They attacked the enemies of philosophy, just as dogs, ready to bark and bite, kept an eye out for their masters' enemies. When Alexander asked him about the origin of his nickname, Diogenes is said to have replied, "I fawn on those who give me something, I bark at those who don't, and sink my teeth into scoundrels."[16]

There are a great many anecdotes of this sort. To Plato, who called him a dog, Diogenes responded, "Very true, for I returned to those who sold me."[17] When guests at a banquet threw him bones, he lifted his leg and urinated on them.[18] Alexander, in a variation on this story, sought to provoke Diogenes by sending him a bowl filled with bones. Diogenes answered that it was "a meal befitting a dog, but not a gift befitting a king."[19]

To properly understand the canine aspect of Cynicism we must examine the paradoxical manner in which dogs were regarded in ancient Greece. Negative stereotypes were common among city dwellers, who saw them as rebels, traitors, ruthless avengers. In a great many contexts, to call someone a dog was a more or less grave insult. More generally, and still more unfavorably, dogs were seen as bloodthirsty beasts, linked in the Greek mind with wolves: they ate raw flesh, and were not always able to distinguish friend from foe; in the worst case, they were capable of indiscriminate violence. In the Homeric poems, they are necrophagous: enemy corpses were thrown—or the threat was made that they would be thrown—to the dogs.[20]

At the same time dogs were valued not only as companions in daily life, but also for the services they could render after death. Some were used to guard the tomb of a defunct master or to accompany him on his final voyage. The funerary monument erected by Diogenes's disciples at Corinth, surmounted by the figure of a dog, testifies to this tradition.

It was exactly the Greeks' familiarity with dogs that gave rise to this ambivalent image and to the pejorative sense of the term "dog," which is found in all societies that welcome dogs into the domestic sphere. No matter that it was an animal, the dog became absorbed into the ethical system of human communities, and perhaps by virtue of this it was either valued or denigrated.[21] In a certain sense, dogs were reproached for their lack of self-control simply because they were the only animals of which self-control was expected. Dogs had a responsibility to be gentle and obedient, faithful and cooperative, capable of telling friends from strangers and adjusting their behavior accordingly. They were to display *aidos*, which is to say they were supposed to show respect for their masters and the members of their households, always acting as circumstances required.

The negative stereotypes associated with dogs in Greek culture therefore arose from a collective anxiety regarding an animal in which great trust was placed. It is against this background that the nickname given to Diogenes must be seen, a name that he himself was to elevate to the status of a philosophical title. In a larger sense, the choice of an animal epithet is consistent with the primacy of the body that Cynic philosophy was dedicated to promoting.

Cynic Attitudes Toward Sexuality

We have seen that the body is inseparable from the elaboration of a Cynic philosophy. For ancients no less than moderns, the doctrines and practices of Diogenes and his followers concerning sexuality are the most puzzling aspect of their legacy.

Any study of Cynic views in this connection immediately runs up against the difficulty that it is not always easy to separate the documentary wheat from the chaff. Many ancient authors, whether they were hostile to Cynicism or simply appalled by the behavior of its exponents, distorted or misrepresented the arguments they made. In the case of Diogenes himself, the rough edges of his thought were frequently smoothed out by his defenders, and its most shocking features toned down or expurgated; his detractors, for their part, called attention to these things in order to blacken his reputation as far as possible. Exaggerated and caricatural treatments of Cynicism are common in works by Epicurean and Christian scholars. Philodemus of Gadara, an Epicurean philosopher of the first century BCE, in his commentary on Diogenes's treatise of political philosophy, the *Republic*,[22] accentuates what he considers to be its most subversive aspects and often presents them in a misleading light. Philodemus claims, for example, that the Cynics reacted violently against anyone who resisted their sexual overtures, contrary to the principle of free consent, a central element of both Cynic and Stoic thought.

A similarly gratuitous reading of Diogenes was popularized by certain Christian authors. The Fathers of the Church were not all of one mind. Whereas some of them—Clement of Alexandria, Origen, and Theodoret of Cyrus—recapitulated Cynic doctrine in a reasonably objective manner, others dwelt to the point of absurdity on the justifications Cynics were supposed to have advanced for incest, parricide, cannibalism, and abandoning burial customs, with the result that they were transformed into monsters, made hideous by every vice imaginable.

One thinks in this connection of Theophilus, bishop of Antioch in the second century CE. Only one book from his hand has come down to us, the *Apology to Autolycus*, in which he seeks to demonstrate the consistency of the Old Testament, contrasting this with what he takes to be the contradictions of the Greek philosophers and, more generally, pagan immorality. The Cynics, he maintained, urged that fathers be cooked and eaten by their children. Other authors extended this type of calumny to the Cynics' heirs, the Stoics. Epiphanius, writing in the fourth century CE, claimed that Zeno endorsed cannibalism; at about the same time John Chrysostom claimed that he made it obligatory.

Other Christian thinkers, less hostile to Diogenes and his followers, reinterpreted those aspects of Cynic tradition they found repugnant. Augustine, for instance, was incapable of believing that the Cynics had sexual relations in public; he convinced himself instead that, even if they had wanted to do so, they were incapable of acting on their desire:

> Here I prefer to think that Diogenes and others who reputedly did such a thing rather acted out the motions of lying together before the eyes of men who really did not know what was done under the cloak. . . . For those philosophers did not blush to seem willing to lie together in a place where lust itself would have blushed to rear its head.[23]

Setting polemical falsifications to one side, what can we conclude about Diogenes's teaching with regard to sexuality? Cynic doctrine considers three types of relation to be permissible: masturbation; sex within marriage, assuming mutual consent; and free love, once again so long as it does not violate the wishes of either person. Free love, taken to its logical conclusion, led Diogenes to approve, as a theoretical matter, all sexual acts observable in nature, including incest, which is found among animals without arousing any objection on their part. Nevertheless, it needs to be emphasized that while Diogenes and his disciples denounced the culturally constructed character of the incest taboo, and while they regarded incest as a natural sexual behavior, they neither advocated it nor practiced it.

Paradoxically, even though Cynics sought to desocialize the sexual act, as it were, by normalizing and trivializing sexual desire, and the manner and the places in which it is satisfied, the Cynic conception of sexuality, excepting the case of masturbation, was based on the idea of mutual consent, which implies the existence of commonly understood codes of social behavior.

Ultimately, Diogenes's argument regarding sexual relations depended on relocating the boundary between public and private, between what is shown and what is hidden, what one does in one's home and what one does in the agora. But reconceiving the distinction between *koinon* (the common, the public, the shared) and *idion* (the private, the particular, the individual) went beyond mere sexual exhibitionism. Diogenes's pupil Crates was in the habit of entering people's homes uninvited and lecturing them; for this he was nicknamed "Door-Opener."[24] Diogenes, as we have seen, held that sexual acts, whether solitary or shared, should be performed for all to see. Crates and his wife, Hipparchia, in keeping with the master's teaching, are said to have had sex together in public on several occasions.[25]

Diogenes on Marriage

Diogenes himself never married, never raised a family. When a friend urged him to have children, he replied that by way of progeny he would leave behind a series of Olympic victories—a remark that can

FIG. 1: Turan Baş, Statue of Diogenes, Sinop, 2006. Height: 5.5 meters. *Wikimedia Commons/Michael F. Schönitzer*

FIG. 2: Commemorative Silver Ten-Euro Coin. National Bank of Greece, 2017. Weight: 34.10 grams; Diameter: 40 millimeters. *Rights Reserved*

FIG. 3: Fresco by David Ghirlandaio, 1475. Vatican Library, Rome. *Wikimedia Commons/Web Gallery of Art*

FIG. 4: Jean-Léon Gérôme, *Diogène* (1860). Walters Museum, Baltimore, inv. 37131; oil on canvas, 74.5 centimeters × 101 centimeters. *Wikimedia Commons/Walters Art Museum*

FIG. 5: John William Waterhouse, *Diogenes* (1882). Art Gallery of New South Wales, Sydney, inv. 720; oil on canvas, 280 centimeters × 134 centimeters. *Wikimedia Commons/Meidosensei*

FIG. 6: Honoré Daumier, *Diogène chiffonnier*, lithograph, in *Le Charivari* (10 July 1842). Musée Carnavalet, Paris, DR 942, Inventaire du fonds français, no. 16. *Roger-Viollet/Musée Carnavalet*

FIG. 7: Diogenes, Detail of the Mosaic of the Seven Philosophers (third century CE). Römisch-Germanisches Museum, Cologne, inv. 8119148399. *Wikimedia Commons/Singinglemon*

FIG. 8: Diogenes in His Barrel, Conversing with a Disciple. Cornelian gemstone (first century BCE). Thorvaldsens Museum, Copenhagen, inv. I 977. 1 × 1.2 centimeters. *Thorvaldsens Museum,* www.thorvaldsensmuseum.dk

FIG. 9: Diogenes in His Barrel. Fragment of an oil lamp, Italy, first century CE. British Museum, London, 1814 0704.174. Length: 5.5 centimeters. Legend: DIOGENES. *Trustees of the British Museum*

FIG. 10: Pierre Puget, *Alexandre et Diogène* (1689). Paris, Musée du Louvre, M. R. 2776, marble relief. 332 centimeters × 296 centimeters × 44 centimeters. *Wikimedia Commons/Siren*

FIG. 11: "Le Tonneau de Diogène," from *Images enfantines* (Paris: Maison Quantin, 1886). 37 centimeters × 27 centimeters. *Musée de l'image, Épinal, France. Rights reserved*

FIG. 12: Housing unit in the form of a barrel, Étang de Mons (Saint Georges Lagricol), France. *Rights reserved*

FIG. 13: Diogenes. Marble bust, late second century CE, origin unknown. Height: 33 centimeters. John Paul Getty Museum, Los Angeles, inv. 73.AA.131. *John Paul Getty Museum*

FIG. 14: The False Stele of Verona, approximately 50 centimeters × 20 centimeters. Museo Maffeiano di Verona, n. inv. della lapide 28697. Photograph by Alfredo Buonopane.

be interpreted variously, but that no doubt indicates that Diogenes wished to enjoy a more lasting posterity than what even a long line of descendants could bring him.[26]

Diogenes's disciples seem to have followed his example in the main. Crates and Hipparchia are the only exception known to us, but their marriage amounted more to a subversion of matrimonial principles than adherence to Greek conjugal norms. Subversion in this case assumed a number of forms, corresponding to the circumstances under which Crates and Hipparchia became engaged, the form of the marriage proposal, the bride's introduction, the nature of their relations, and the marriages of the children born of their union.[27]

Marriage in ancient Greece typically involved the transfer of property or money. The bride's father chose his son-in-law and gave his daughter's hand in marriage together with a dowry. Usually, then, the young woman had no say in the choice of her husband. Not so with Hipparchia. Having fallen in love with Crates, she threatened to kill herself if her parents did not allow her to marry him.

The matrimonial ritual required the bride to unveil herself before her new family, showing her hair to persons who once were strangers and now were intimates. Crates daringly reversed the terms of this gesture and turned it to his own advantage, standing naked before the woman who wished to marry him. Diogenes Laertius gives this account:

> [Crates] stood up, took off his clothes in front of her, and said, "This is the bridegroom, and this is his property. Think it over! For you will be no companion for me unless you adopt my way of life."[28]

Moreover, not only did Crates and Hipparchia make love in public, but Hipparchia, contrary to custom, accompanied Crates at banquets.

In seeking to undermine the familiar conception of matrimony, Crates also called upon the services of his children with Hipparchia.

The dramatist Menander, his contemporary, says in the *Twin Sisters* that, in a flagrant breach of proper conduct, he gave his daughter in marriage for a trial period of thirty days.[29] Similarly, when his son Pasicles had completed his military service, Crates took him to a prostitute and told him that she was the sort of woman he was to marry.[30]

Apart from the isolated case of Crates and Hipparchia, Cynic doctrine categorically rejected marriage and advocated total sexual freedom. This amounted to heresy in a society where marriage, entered into for the purpose of producing children, was considered to be a civic duty. Children, once grown, were expected in their turn to conclude matrimonial alliances with other families, and later to take care of their parents in old age (an obligation known as *gērotrophia*), to arrange for funeral ceremonies after their death, and to take responsibility for the transmission of the family patrimony.

The institution of marriage, in other words, was a cornerstone of the social structure of ancient Greece; indeed, its significance can be seen in the vocabulary used to refer to bachelors, known as *agamoi*, literally "the ununited, the unmarried." The condition of not being married, and especially of not having produced offspring to whom one's estate and social standing could be lawfully passed on, was a proof of disrepute. In Athens, to reproach an adversary for being single was a familiar courtroom tactic used to depict someone as a poor citizen. Demosthenes, for instance, in his speech *Against Olympiodorus*, attacked his opponent in these terms: "For you must know, men of the jury, that this fellow Olympiodorus has never married an Athenian woman in accordance with your laws; he has no children nor has ever had any."[31]

Some cities seem to have gone further than others in condemning avoidance of marriage; in Sparta, we are told, discriminatory laws were adopted against bachelors above a certain age. It is not hard to understand why Diogenes, in rejecting the institution of matrimony, should have acted as he did. Asked when was the right moment to marry, he replied, "For a young man, not yet; for an old man, never at all."[32] He praised those who, on the verge of getting married, thought better of it, and those who, on the verge of having children, elected to remain childless. An Arabic papyrus reports that Diogenes, seeing a young man ask for a lady's hand in marriage, commented, "A brief distraction leading to many problems."[33]

Men stood little to gain in the way of sexual freedom from Cynic arguments, it would appear, since male sexual freedom was already very considerable in Greek cities during Diogenes's time. Men were able, depending on their desire and means, to have sex with male or female prostitutes, also with household slaves and whatever young men they were able to seduce. Only relations with the wife of a citizen or with a young woman engaged to be married were considered adulterous and punished by the law on this ground. By contrast, the freedom Cynic philosophy offered women was novel, and much broader in scope than anything other schools had proposed up until then.

Beyond the sexual aspects of his doctrine, Diogenes, in arguing against marriage, rejected the family unit and, more generally, the idea of community life. Associations of all types, particularly religious institutions, were numerous in the cities of his age and played a large part in the construction of personal identities. Breaking free of these arrangements, in keeping with the Cynic position regarding *philia* and civic attachments, amounted to dismissing the very idea of social allegiance. Cosmopolitanism was merely the logical extension of this position: in Diogenes's eyes, the only legitimate form of communal belonging was membership in the human race.

But if Diogenes was remarkable for his opposition to conjugality, his understanding of the function it served scarcely differed from that of his contemporaries. Like them, he saw marriage as a mechanism for carrying on the paternal line while transmitting family wealth to successive generations, and looked upon children primarily as heirs and secondarily as a source of support in old age. The life of mendicancy that Diogenes chose therefore denied the social usefulness of offspring and broke with the ideal of intergenerational solidarity that marriage represented: rearing legitimate descendants and then waiting until the time came for children to take care of their parents, feeding them and finally putting them in the ground. When someone asked him who would carry him out to be buried after he died, Diogenes replied, "Whoever wants my house."[34]

Just as his implicit conception of marriage was traditional, his opinion of adultery did not depart from the norm. Once more an anecdote illustrates the point. On learning that a flute player named Didymon had been convicted of adultery, Diogenes recommended—in a play on words of the sort he was so fond of— that the man be hanged by his name (the term *didumoi*, meaning "that which is double" and therefore, by extension, "twins," was used metaphorically to refer to testicles).[35] Diogenes's approval of physical punishment in the case of adultery was consistent yet again with the practice of the times: in Athens, male adulterers were depilated with ashes and then subjected to *rhaphanidōsis*, which is to say anal penetration with a turnip; in the aftermath of this infamous ritual they were mocked for being "wide-assed" (*euryproktoi*).

To Diogenes's way of thinking, then, adultery constituted evidence of intemperance, a close cousin of gluttony and drunkenness. "There is nothing more vile," he is reported to have said, "than the adulterer who gives up his soul in exchange for venal commodities."[36] But if Diogenes's position in the matter of adultery was conventional, his views on pederasty and prostitution, two of the main variants of masculine sexuality, were by no means widely shared.

Diogenes on Pederasty

It is well known that men in various parts of ancient Greece enjoyed sexual relations not only with adult female partners, but also with boys and young men. This latter type of relation, called pederasty if it was not engaged in with a prostitute, combined political education, amorous feeling, and sexual intimacy in variable proportions.

Diogenes, unlike his teacher Antisthenes, seems not to have given himself up to this pleasure; our sources mention only relations with courtesans. He was chiefly concerned to monitor the behavior of boys and young men and warn them against the danger of being taken advantage of by ill-intentioned adults. His interest in the youth of the cities through which he passed, in other words, appears to have been that of a tutor rather than of a consumer. Thus to a handsome fellow on his way to a drinking party, Diogenes said, "You will come back a worse man." The next day the young man told him, "I went and am none the worse for it." Diogenes crudely replied, "Worse, no; but wider [*eurytiōn*], yes."[37] Similarly, noticing a good-looking lad asleep in public view, Diogenes "nudged him and said, 'Wake up! Lest someone fix a spear in your back while you sleep.'"[38] And again, seeing a young man studying philosophy, he congratulated Philosophy herself, saying, "Well done! You're turning lovers of the body's beauty toward [the] beauty of [the] mind."[39] In a certain sense, Diogenes adopted a paternalistic attitude toward these young men, and seems to have shared the anxieties of parents who, according to Plato, had their young boys guarded and accompanied by slave teachers, "to prevent them from being looked after by lovers."[40]

Diogenes on Prostitutes

Diogenes's argument in connection with prostitution is more complicated. Clearly he saw female prostitutes as enemies of self-sufficiency and independence. The desires they arouse and the cycle of sexual longing they set in motion condemn men to a sort of incontinence. Consider the account of Diogenes's visit to Delphi and his contemplation of the golden statue of Aphrodite sponsored by Phryne, one of the most famous courtesans of the fourth century, remembered for her beauty and her many wealthy lovers. She served as Praxiteles's model for the *Aphrodite of Knidos*. When she was brought to trial on a capital charge, her lawyer, the orator Hypereides (himself one of her lovers), fearing an unfavorable verdict, famously removed her robe, exposing her breasts to the jurors in the hope of winning her acquittal.

The statue dedicated by Phryne seemed to Diogenes to be a memorial to the state of dependence into which men had been reduced, not by her alone, but by all whores of her kind. He is said to have engraved upon the base this legend: "With the compliments of Greek licentiousness"—a trenchant summary of his views on the subject.[41] He was well familiar with female sex workers. Prostitutes and courtesans were so numerous in Athens and Corinth that the verb *korinthazein*, constructed from the name of the second of these port cities, was used to designate sexual commerce; recourse to their services was considered perfectly normal. Moreover, they represented an alternative source of sexual gratification that was particularly welcomed by young men, who were forbidden to have contact with the majority of young women their age. But Diogenes, indifferent to the utility of prostitution in the general economy of the matrimonial system, mistrusted courtesans and their power over men. He regretted that so many men slavishly obeyed them, comparing temptresses like Phryne to a lethal sweet beverage.[42] Even so, he did not underestimate the value of prostitution as an opportunity for philosophical instruction. According to Plutarch, he advised his listeners to go into any brothel in order to learn that "there is no difference between what costs money and what costs nothing."[43]

Diogenes himself frequented Lais of Hyccara, one of the most sought-after courtesans of the fourth century in Corinth. If the sources that have come down to us are to be believed, their relations were not of a commercial nature. Aristippus, by contrast, a philosophical rival who founded the Cyrenaic school, paid for Lais's services and took her with him for two months every year to Aegina during the festival of Poseidon, provoking Diogenes's scorn.[44]

Diogenes, Social Conservative

Nevertheless, the revolutionary character of Diogenes's sexual doctrine should not be overstated. He and his disciples continued to propagate rather traditional values as well, particularly with regard to gender assignment. Diogenes reproached a young man who was behaving effeminately for thinking he could improve on nature's work: having been made a man, he wished to become a woman.[45] Similarly, on meeting a young man whose chin was shaved, he asked, "So you've got a complaint against nature, because it made you a man rather than a woman?"[46]

Nor was the principle of gender asymmetry objected to. On several occasions Diogenes expressed his contempt for men who allowed themselves to be penetrated by other men (*kinaidoi*). When a young man dressed as a woman put a question to him, Diogenes refused to reply until he pulled up his robe to show whether he was a woman or a man.[47] For Diogenes, it was the man who penetrated and the woman who was penetrated. And even though he went on over the course of his career to argue in favor of the equality of men and women in respect of virtue, when he cited exemplary mythological figures, women were seldom held up as models. Two rare sources of feminine inspiration seem to have been Niobe and Medea. According to Philo of Alexandria, when the philosopher was imprisoned, malnourished, and waiting to be sold into slavery, Diogenes sought to encourage a despondent companion to join him in eating what little was given them, quoting these verses from the *Iliad*:

> Even Niobe with her lustrous hair remembered food, though she saw a dozen children killed in her own halls, six daughters and six sons in the pride and prime of youth.[48]

Niobe, in his eyes, was the symbol par excellence of resilience. By Amphion she had given birth to an equal number of daughters and sons (six or seven, depending on the source). But Leto, angered by her pride, and having only two children herself, a daughter and a son, Artemis and Apollo, sent them to kill Niobe's children.

In much the same way, Diogenes saw Medea, niece of the sorceress Circe, as a benign figure rather than a poisoner:

> She took weak men with bodies ruined by flabbiness, made them sweat it off in the palaestra and the bathhouse and in this way made them strong and vigorous. This is why she is said to have roasted human flesh in order to make it youthful once more.[49]

Diogenes, in rationalizing the myth, made Medea's murder of Pelias the result of mythographic distortion.

By comparison with these positive references, among the very few known to us, misogynous apothegms are legion. Antonius and Maximus the Confessor report that, on coming across two women who were chatting, Diogenes observed, "The adder borrows poison from the viper."[50] In the same vein, a pair of apothegms preserved in the notebook of a Greek schoolboy in Egypt have come down to us that unambiguously reveal the feeling that women typically inspired in the philosopher:

> Seeing two women enjoying each other's company, he said, "The scorpion obtains poison from a spider."
>
> Noticing a woman learning to read and write, he said, "She is sharpening a sword."[51]

If Diogenes mistrusted women, and took as much pleasure in misogynous witticisms as other men of his time did, he nonetheless did not approve of the customary forms of male amusement. In particular, he took a critical view of the principal form of elite masculine sociability, the banquet (*symposion*) or private dinner party.

Diogenes at the Banquet

Diogenes's relationship to this institution was a complicated one. On the one hand, he regarded banquets as a setting for philosophical activity, where he could engage in debate with a view to persuading a sophisticated audience; but at the same time, from an ethical point of view, he despised them as the supreme embodiment of useless pleasures. In spite of his penury, Diogenes seems not to have seen banquets as a way of eating at little or no expense, nor was he perpetually on the lookout for a new place to spend his evenings. If Plutarch can be believed, he preferred to curl up in a corner of the marketplace and go to sleep just when night-long festivities were getting under way.[52] In this he set himself apart from parasites, the name that Athenians gave to those who went from one party to the next in search of free food and drink. Both mendicants and parasites nonetheless violated the principle of reciprocity. At one banquet Diogenes was amused to see a mouse jump up onto his table. "Lo and behold!" he cried. "Even Diogenes keeps parasites!"[53]

Aristocratic dinner parties were the perfect example of everything he objected to in the way of luxury and excess—in a word, all that was unnecessary, superfluous. The symposium was compounded of a variety of entertainments: performances by acrobats and dancers, music, poetry readings, philosophical debate, and sex. Wine played an essential role. Antonius and Maximus, in their treatise *On Sobriety*, recount an episode that illustrates the discrepancy between the values that Diogenes promoted and the ones celebrated by the guests at these parties:

> During one banquet, Diogenes poured on the ground a cupful of wine that had been poured rather too generously. When some of the guests reproached him for this, he replied, "Had I drunk it, not only would the wine have disappeared but it would have done away with me as well!"[54]

The hostility he faced on such occasions is unmistakable. At the same time, Diogenes's ambivalence toward the banquet as an elite recreation cannot be fully appreciated unless it is placed in the context of Cynic thinking about the body.

The Body as a Philosophical Coat of Arms

With Diogenes, the body became a means of expressing a philosophical choice and a conviction, which is to say a mode of demonstration that was worth more than any treatise. In this he carried on the tradition of Socrates and Antisthenes, particularly with regard to clothing: neither one wore a tunic or sandals, only a simple cloak.

The Cynics invented a particular style by folding the cloak. According to some authors, Diogenes was the first to do this; according to others, he did it at Antisthenes's suggestion, after having asked him for a tunic; still others attribute the innovation to Diodorus of Aspendus.[55]

The tunic was standard dress in summer; when winter came, it was combined with a cloak. The Cynics preferred to use only the cloak, in this way advertising their contempt for comfort. When the cold became intense, they simply folded the cloak upon itself, creating a double layer, without the addition of any other article of clothing. At night, in winter, they used it as a covering; in summer, as a mattress. In so doing, Diogenes and his followers once again departed from convention, according to which not only one's dress, but also one's general appearance, was supposed to declare one's social standing. The Cynics, by following Socrates in choosing a life of simplicity (*euteleia*) and material poverty, gave added emphasis to the symbolic reversal this implied. But the reversal had its limits. There may have been an element of vanity in wearing an old robe whose holes and tears constituted so many outward signs of philosophical commitment. Plato, for example, frequently mocked Antisthenes for his insistence on calling attention to the most worn parts of a thread-bare cloak.[56]

The Cynics therefore had a uniform: in addition to the cloak, they carried a walking stick and a wallet, that is, a leather traveling bag or knapsack—emblems of the itinerant condition of mendicant philosophers. They were an indispensable part of the Cynics' everyday life, so much so that, as Diogenes put it, the word "impaired" (*anapérous*) ought to be applied not to the deaf and the blind, but to those who have no knapsack (*pēra*).[57] In the same vein, Crates said that what he gained from philosophy was a quart of lupine seeds and the absence of care.[58] The following mock-Homeric lines in praise of the Cynics' knapsack are attributed to him:

> There is a city, Pera, in the middle of a wine-dark mist,
> Lovely and fertile, rich in dirt, possessing nothing,
> Into which sails neither stupid parasite
> nor glutton exulting in the buttocks of a harlot;
> Instead it bears thyme and garlic and figs and loaves,
> For the sake of which men do not fight each other,
> Nor take up arms for fame or fortune.[59]

Apart from Diogenes's costume and accessories, the very little information we have regarding his physical appearance amounts more to a stereotype than a realistic portrait. Sidonius Apollinaris, a Gallo-Roman aristocrat and man of letters writing in the fifth century CE, briefly mentions the appearance not of the philosopher himself, but of the statues commemorating him. In a letter to Faustus, the bishop of Riez, he enumerates the distinctive features of the statues of various philosophers:

> Speusippus with his head bowed forward, Aratus with his head bent back, Zeno with knitted brow, Epicurus with unwrinkled skin, *Diogenes with long beard*, Socrates with trailing hair, Aristotle with out-thrust arm; Xenocrates with gathered leg, Heraclitus with eyes

closed through weeping, Democritus with lips wide open with
laughter, Chrysippus with fingers bent to denote counting, Euclid
with fingers extended because of the size of his measurements,
Cleanthes with fingers gnawed for both reasons.[60]

Diogenes seems therefore to have regularly been portrayed by
sculptors in marble and bronze as having a full beard (*barba comans*).
This is the beard one sees in a marble bust from the imperial period
conserved at the Getty Museum (Fig. 13). The treatment is clearly
typological. There are hints of a more detailed physical description, beyond the familiar emphasis on Diogenes's hirsuteness, from
ancient sources. Epictetus says he was short, stocky, glowing with
health.[61] Sextus Empiricus, for his part, indicates that, contrary to
custom, Diogenes went about with one shoulder bare.[62] In the icon-
ographic tradition, he is frequently shown to be bald.

The modesty of Diogenes's dress coincides with the sympathy he
expressed on many occasions for the Spartan mode of life, which he
knew well from his time in Laconia.

Diogenes, Laconophile

The cultivation of simplicity in all things naturally attracted Diogenes
to Sparta, the Greek city of his time that was most frequently associated with this virtue, and all the more in view of the emphasis
he placed on strengthening both body and mind. His very taste for
short sentences and pithy retorts was in keeping with the local habit
of speaking tersely—an ideal that came to be known, aptly enough,
as laconism. The treatment of men and women, less asymmetrical in
Sparta than elsewhere, likewise suited him temperamentally.

Diogenes was not alone in his fascination with Sparta. Many
public figures in Athens had come under its spell in the preceding

century. Cimon, Pericles's chief political rival, is no doubt the most famous example. But laconophilia assumed a number of different forms. Some admired the model of the Spartan citizen-soldier; others, the Spartan constitution; still others, the Spartan way of life, and particularly the association of gymnastic training with communal meals, as well as austerity with regard to food and clothing. It was this last aspect of Spartan culture, the value placed upon frugality, self-reliance, and strength, that appealed to Diogenes. Making his way once to Athens from Lacedaemon, in response to someone who asked where he had come from and where he was going, he said, "From the men's quarters to the women's."[63]

Nevertheless, he did not spare Sparta from all criticism. When someone inquired where he found good men in Greece, he replied, "Good men nowhere, but good lads in Sparta."[64] The plan of education Diogenes devised for the children of Xeniades, his Corinthian master, resembled a Spartan upbringing in many respects: frugal diet, hair cut short, no article of clothing other than a cloak, bare feet, the habit of walking in silence with eyes lowered, and practice in hunting.

In setting Athens against Sparta, a common theme in writings of the period, Diogenes seems to have followed the example of Antisthenes. According to Aristotle, Antisthenes called taverns (*kapēleia*) the mess tables (*phitidia*) of Attica—this last the term habitually used to refer to the meals shared by Spartan citizen-soldiers.[65] Comparing Athenian taverns, raucous places of entertainment and relaxation, with the sober eating halls of Sparta was a way, stereotypically, of contrasting a city of laxity and self-indulgence with one of self-restraint and discipline.

The reasons for which Diogenes praised Spartan physical culture were similar to those that led him to criticize the cult of athletics that had grown up in other Greek cities.

The Critique of Athletics

Diogenes was very familiar with the world of sports and frequently borrowed images from it. Thus he compared human existence to a competition in which one cannot let up before the end:

> To those who said, "You're an old man, take it easy from now on," he would reply, "If I were running a distance race, would I slow down when approaching the finishing line? Wouldn't I do better to speed up?"[66]

I mentioned earlier that Diogenes attended both the Olympic and the Isthmian games. We may be certain that, as a scion of the upper class in Sinope, he had himself been trained in the various athletic disciplines, especially running and wrestling, the two pillars of physical education for young boys. Stobaeus reports this apothegm: "I have seen many men competing in wrestling and running, but no one competing [in the pursuit of] human excellence."[67]

He had also been trained in boxing, if we can credit the anecdote reported by Diogenes Laertius, who says that after having been assaulted by one Meidias, he got a pair of leather gloves the next day and gave his tormentor a thrashing.[68] Yet the advantages an athletic education might seem to have given him did not prevent Diogenes from lamenting its consequences. He was not the first to have been disturbed by the admiration reserved for sporting champions. An early critic was Xenophanes of Colophon, in the sixth century, who objected to what he saw as the excessive praise showered upon triumphant athletes by their native cities. Statues were erected, odes were composed in their honor, privileges of various types were granted, including monetary rewards and the right to be fed at the city's expense. Among Diogenes's contemporaries, Plato and Aristotle deplored the veneration of athletics, as Euripides had done before them.

Diogenes, for his part, took aim at the symbolic system created and perpetuated by sporting competitions. He disputed the effectiveness of games in promoting health, and for this reason forbade the teacher of wrestling and gymnastics hired by Xeniades from teaching his children athletic exercises, allowing him to demonstrate only those that heightened their color and kept them fit.[69] Furthermore, he disdained the energy that was put into sports, especially wrestling, arguing that it should be directed instead to producing virtue: "Men strive in digging and kicking to outdo one another," he said, "but no one strives to become a good man and true."[70]

Similarly, he insisted on the uselessness of the training regimen followed by athletes, with its emphasis on regulating dietary and sexual activity for the purpose of optimizing performance. He criticized the cult of muscular development and the unhealthy consequences of a meat-based diet, instituted a century and a half earlier. Asked why athletes were stupid, he replied, "Because they are built up of mutton and beef."[71] Likewise, he mocked the obsession with winning as a form of slavery, and dismissed the strength of character that sports claimed to instill as an illusion, noting that it melts away at the sight of a shapely woman, as in the case of the pankratiast Dioxippus, overcome by desire for a young prostitute just as he was making his triumphal entry into Athens.[72]

And yet there is no rejection of the body in Cynicism. The Cynic conception of ascesis was not motivated by contempt for the flesh; still less did it spring from a hatred of bodily passions and appetites, accompanied by a will to mortification. Instead the body was thought of as a means of philosophical education. Self-discipline in respect of the soul was closely linked to self-discipline in respect of the body: not only were the two mutually reinforcing, but without the one the other was not possible. The philosopher was required to maintain good health, to harden himself physically, to improve his

powers of resistance in order to withstand any challenge. Diogenes
Laertius put the matter this way:

> [Diogenes held that] training was twofold, encompassing both
> mind and body; that in the case of physical training, ideals are
> engendered that foster the suppleness needed to perform virtuous
> deeds; and that neither facet was complete without the other, since
> health and strength are equally essential for training both the mind
> and the body.[73]

The concern with good health is very much a part of Cynic thought.
Diogenes himself chided his contemporaries for neglecting it.
According to Athenodorus, his glowing appearance came from rubbing his body with fragrant oil.[74] Instead of anointing his head, as
was the custom, he anointed his feet, remarking humorously that
from his head the fragrance passed into the air, but from his feet it
went into his nostrils.[75]

But if Diogenes contested the benefits of athletic competition, by
virtue of just this he displayed a deep acquaintance with the world
of sports. He was, after all, a man of the fourth century. In criticizing
games and the people who played them, he testified to the vitality of
athletic culture in the Greece of his time and to the fascination that
its champions exerted over urban populations—a source of chronic
exasperation among philosophers, physicians, and poets. Diogenes,
though he shared their dismay, nonetheless reappropriated certain
standard gymnasium exercises for his own purposes. Two examples
stand out.

Statues in gymnasiums were used by athletes to develop various
physical abilities, useful in grappling with opponents, for example, or
supporting weight, all with a view to increasing muscular strength.
Diogenes adopted the same regimen, only with a quite different objective, waiting until winter to embrace the statues, when they were
covered with snow, and in this way testing his powers of endurance
in the cold. This was a matter not of looking to exploit a narrowly

athletic advantage, but of enlarging a more general capacity for perseverance, which the Greeks called *karteria*.

In a similar way, wrestling exercises in the palaestra, on trodden earth and sand that had been sifted to cushion falls, were turned to another purpose by Diogenes: he waited until summer, when the sand was burning, before rolling in it, the better to be able to endure heat. In so doing, he transformed athletic training into a philosophical discipline. His disciple Crates, who likewise sought to harden himself against seasonal changes in the weather, favored more traditional methods, wearing a thick cloak in the summer and a tattered cloak in the winter.[76]

Nevertheless, Diogenes was not concerned only with his own health. He wished also to educate all those around him.

Chapter 4

Diogenes, Mentor

[Diogenes] was entering a theater as everyone else was leaving it; when asked why he did so, he replied, "This is what I have been doing all my life." When people laughed at him for walking backwards under the public arcade, he said to them, "Aren't you ashamed to blame me for walking backwards, when you are walking in the wrong direction your whole life through?"

The first episode is reported by Diogenes Laertius,[1] the second by Johannes Stobaeus.[2] These two moments neatly summarize his unfailing determination to go against the current of society and conventional opinion. But with Diogenes, unlike Socrates, there was no room for politeness when it came to attaining virtue: he deliberately sought to give offense. This was philosophy with no holds barred. His rejection of the dominant methods for transmitting knowledge in the Greece of his time, whether in the form of written dialogues or speeches by recognized authorities, was complete. There was nothing at all restrained about Diogenes's behavior. He is said, for example, to have disrupted a lecture by Anaximenes of Lampsacus by brandishing a salted fish, not only to distract the attention of the audience but also to ridicule the rhetorician's outsized appetite.[3] Diogenes meant to shock—and in this way to make people argue with one another. He assigned himself the role of educator, not only with regard to his disciples, but also and above all with regard to all those he met with in the course of his travels.

A Mad Socrates

Diogenes was intent on talking to people in the places where they lived and worked. In this he set himself apart from the masters of other philosophical schools, who gave instruction in places dedicated to education and conducive to study, after the example of the gymnasium of the Academy, where Plato taught. Socrates had anticipated Diogenes in making the city his domain. But if Diogenes followed Socrates in looking to convert interlocutors to philosophy, he did not apply the same methods. Plato, who knew both men, famously remarked that Diogenes was "Socrates gone mad" (*mainomenos*)—a phrase that implicitly acknowledged elements of continuity between the two thinkers.[4] The grammarian Marcus Cornelius Fronto, in the second century CE, observed that while both Socrates and Diogenes were forceful and serious in manner, they practiced philosophy in quite different ways, Socrates adopting a courteous and affable style of speaking, by contrast with the intemperate language and brutal attacks to which Diogenes was given.[5] The two men were regularly compared, to the point that sometimes they were confused with each other. This would surely have displeased Diogenes, who took a rather dim view of Socrates, accusing him of having lived a life of luxury (he owned a little house, furnished with a couch, and he wore sandals from time to time).[6]

However much he may have wished to distance himself from the first of his two great models, did Diogenes nonetheless carry on the Socratic tradition, as the heir not only of Socrates himself but also of his pupil Antisthenes?

Diogenes as Founder

To put the matter another way: was Diogenes the father of Cynicism, or must the honor be granted to Antisthenes, who is said to have been his teacher? The question of priority has been the subject of debate since antiquity. It is a matter of some consequence for the history of philosophy, because the connection between the Stoics and Socratic thought depends indirectly on the nature of the Cynic succession.

Three lines of descent have been identified: Socrates was the teacher of Antisthenes, Diogenes was the teacher of Crates, and Crates was the teacher of Zeno, the founder of Stoicism. If Diogenes was indeed Antisthenes's pupil, their relationship constitutes the link permitting the Stoics to claim a Socratic filiation, by virtue of the following chain of transmission: Socrates–Antisthenes–Diogenes–Crates–Zeno. Diogenes Laertius, our principal source on this phase in the development of Greek philosophy, endorses such a sequence, having structured the sixth and seventh books of his *Lives of the Eminent Philosophers* in accordance with a continuist model.[7]

But establishing that Diogenes did in fact study under Antisthenes runs up against chronological obstacles. When he came to Athens, Diogenes met many of Socrates's friends, Antisthenes among them, according to Dio Chrysostom, together with Plato, Aristippus, Aeschines, and Euclid of Megara. Xenophon was no longer in Athens by this point, having been sentenced to exile in 399, the year of Socrates's death, following his participation in the campaign to aid Cyrus. "It was not long before [Diogenes] despised all of them," Dio says, "save Antisthenes."[8] Diogenes was reputed to have been his sole pupil. Several sources maintain that Diogenes alone managed to overcome Antisthenes's reluctance; only after exposing himself to the risk of physical harm was he finally allowed to receive instruction. Diogenes Laertius reports that when Antisthenes raised his staff against him, "Diogenes offered his head and said, 'Strike, for you'll not find wood hard enough to keep me away from you, as long as I think you have something to say.' "[9]

The information available to us regarding Antisthenes's dates is connected in part with events of military history. He fought in the Battle of Tanagra in 426, which implies that he was born, at the latest, around 446–445. More than a half-century later, he commented on the result of the Battle of Leuctra, which took place in 371. According to Plutarch, Antisthenes, on seeing the Thebans boast of their victory over the Spartans, said that they resembled little boys proud of having given their tutor a beating.[10] Diodorus Siculus, for his part, indicates that Antisthenes was still alive in 366.[11] He was then at least eighty years old and, assuming our information is correct, very probably died shortly afterward.

Diogenes Laertius recounts an episode from the last months of Antisthenes's life, when he was very sick: Diogenes gave Antisthenes a dagger to kill himself with, and Antisthenes refused.[12] We should nonetheless treat this story with caution, for no document not directly concerned with the relationship between the two men attests to Diogenes's presence in Athens before 366.

However this may be, even if a relationship between the two men remains purely conjectural, there can be no doubt that Diogenes was able to acquaint himself with Antisthenes's thought, if only through his writings, which plainly had a strong influence on his own philosophy, whether or not a line of intellectual descent passed through him directly to the Stoics. There is much of Antisthenes in Diogenes: the insistence on virtue as the philosopher's chief aim, and the precedence of virtue over the laws, customs, and conventions of Greek cities; the primacy of deeds by comparison with ideas, which were, at most, of secondary importance; and the equality of men and women, or least of their virtues. But Diogenes developed his philosophy as much in opposition to Plato as in agreement with Antisthenes.

Diogenes Versus Plato

Diogenes had nothing but contempt for Plato, who was some twenty-five years his elder. Other prominent figures were the object of his abuse, not only Socrates but Euripides as well; the cruelest barbs, however, he reserved for the founder of the Academy. In this he carried on a quarrel begun by Antisthenes, who, while he seems never actually to have fallen out with Plato, was unsparing in his criticism of him. Antisthenes attacked Plato in a lost dialogue, the *Sathōn*. The title plays on the rhyme of *Platōn* with *Sathōn*, derived from the noun *sathē*, designating the penis or the foreskin. By itself, the title warns the reader against expecting anything in the way of praise.

Diogenes's principal disagreement with Plato had to do with what he saw as a culpable discrepancy between what he taught and how he lived. One apothegm may stand for many in this regard: "Those who utter fine words but don't act on them resemble a harp."[13] Just as the lyre does not hear the sounds it produces, Plato was deaf to the practical implication of his own arguments. He was a philosopher of words, not of deeds—which is to say an imposter.

Diogenes heaped scorn on the theory of Ideas and the related notion, in the *Republic*, of an Ideal City. Plato's famous definition of man as a featherless biped he found risible. Annoyed by the applause it won him, Diogenes retaliated by plucking a cock and bringing it to the lecture hall at the Academy, saying to the audience, "Here is Plato's man!"[14]

He caricatured Plato as an incorrigible chatterbox, mocked his ostentatious generosity, castigated him for the unnecessary comforts of his home, and called his school a waste of time (playing on the Greek words *diatribē* [lectures] and *katatribē* [wasting of time]).[15] Self-interest was Plato's only real interest, he complained; making matters worse, Plato took care not to give offense. Themistius, a Sophist of the fourth century CE, reports Diogenes's exaspera-tion: "Of what use for us is a man who, although he has long practised philosophy, has never yet upset anyone?"[16]

Diogenes sought to discredit not only the Platonic conception of education, but, more generally, the view of higher education shared by the various schools of philosophy. Whereas Plato considered that fifty years were needed to train a philosopher, who had to successfully pass through a great many phases of instruction, Diogenes and the Cynic school regarded the practice of philosophy as something that should be taken up immediately. It was for this reason that the Stoic philosopher Apollodorus of Seleucia, in the second century BCE, described Cynic education as "a shortcut to virtue."[17] On this view, access to philosophical competence was to be achieved by practical application, by acts rather than words; what is more, the life of the philosopher had to be entered into without delay or precondition. It was for this latter reason that some modern commentators have characterized the Cynic attitude as existentialist. From this there arose a desire on the part of Diogenes and his followers, if not to turn their backs on culture and knowledge completely, at least to disregard certain fields of learning altogether.

Speaking Freely

By contrast with the traditional view of philosophical education, as a matter mainly of acquiring knowledge for the purpose of transmitting it from one generation to the next, Diogenes laid emphasis on the paramount importance of self-awareness, which depended on speaking one's mind at all costs. With Diogenes this practice assumed several forms, all of them hurtful: insult, reprimand, and sarcasm.

The Greeks called this style of self-expression by the name of *parrhēsia*. It was Diogenes who made it the cornerstone of the conduct of a Cynic philosopher. When asked what was the most beautiful thing in the world, he replied, "Freedom of speech!"[18] Epictetus, considering the moral qualities of Diogenes and his followers, remarked that frankness was to the Cynics what arms and bodyguards were to kings and tyrants.[19] Indeed, Diogenes made *parrhēsia* a way of life, to the great displeasure of those whom he came into contact with. Diogenes Laertius reports many of Diogenes's insulting remarks and scathing rejoinders, often directed at individuals but sometimes meant to admonish a crowd. One day he called for people to gather around him, and then lashed out at them with his staff, saying, "It was men I was calling for, not trash."[20] Similarly, on meeting an untalented lyre player whose audience always deserted him, Diogenes hailed him with the words "Greetings, rooster!" When the musician asked why he addressed him in this way, Diogenes replied, "Because when you sing you make everyone get up."[21]

Sarcasm was not infrequently substituted for cruelty. Of a philosopher learnedly discoursing on celestial phenomena, Diogenes inquired how long it had taken him to come down from the sky.[22] More than once he tactlessly poked fun at Anaximenes for his obesity: "Give us beggars something of your paunch; for your load will be lightened, and you'll do us a good turn."[23]

It was by engaging in debate with the inhabitants of the cities through which he passed that Diogenes promoted his philosophy. And these encounters, owing to his quite remarkable rudeness, were not without risk of physical injury. With Diogenes, philosophy became transformed into a combat sport.

Occupational Hazards

The Cynic philosopher's existence was compounded of a great many discomforts. Having to beg for food, with no home and only a rough cloak to keep warm in winter, with no friends or family, it was a hard life.

Living outdoors, Diogenes was exposed to the elements. The rain often left him soaking wet. Plato saw this as proof of his pride and craving for glory.[24] But above all Diogenes exposed himself to attacks of every kind. He was sworn at, tripped up and sent sprawling, beaten. Nevertheless, he was not the first philosopher to suffer physically as a result of his teaching. Socrates was occasionally punched and had his hair pulled. Diogenes seems very frequently to have been subject to indignities of this kind. Merchants assaulted him for overturning their wares; young revelers for appearing at a drinking party with his head half shaved.[25] The threat of violence was a constant worry. When someone hit him in the head, he cried, "Heracles! How could I have forgotten to wear my helmet?"[26] An Arabic papyrus preserves an anonymous piece of advice: "Beware of the back streets of town, people are hiding in the shadows, ready to lay into you."[27]

But unlike Socrates, who chose to ignore his tormentors, Diogenes could not help but respond. Following the attack on him at the banquet, he wrote down on a tablet the names of those who had struck him and went about with it hung around his neck, until finally they became objects of public opprobrium.[28] On another occasion he reacted violently after having been assaulted by a wealthy Athenian named Meidias, who was in the habit of committing this type of offense. Known for having clashed with Demosthenes for personal and political reasons, Meidias is remembered for having punched the great orator in the face at the Great Dionysia festival in 348.[29] Diogenes, for his part, would not allow such insolence to go unpunished, and the next day paid back his aggressor in his own coin.[30]

As chronic victims of physical violence or verbal abuse—jeered at the theater, maligned in the Assembly, attacked in the courts— ancient Greek thinkers practiced "a dangerous profession," to recall the title of Luciano Canfora's book.[31] At the same time, and without there being any contradiction in this, Diogenes, a familiar figure of everyday life in Athens and Corinth, seems to have been regarded with respect, and even something like affection, by a great many. I mentioned earlier that when a young boy broke the jar that served him as a home, on the edge of the Agora, the Athenians punished the lad and approved the use of public funds to provide Diogenes with a new jar.[32]

The City as Lecture Hall

Following in Socrates's footsteps, Diogenes made the city his classroom. Wherever he went he engaged in conversation: in the public square and the buildings that surrounded it (the Metröon in Athens, for example, in the shadow of which he had installed his jar), in the main streets and under the arcades, where he enjoyed walking, debating, casting dice or knucklebones; also in the gymnasia, where young athletes trained. No doubt he was not always welcome. His disciple Crates frequented the same places and with the same intentions. Diogenes Laertius tells us that once, in his native city of Thebes, Crates was flogged by the master of a gymnasium and dragged out by his heels.[33]

Diogenes neglected no opportunity for philosophical education: sanctuaries, baths, barber and cobbler shops, taverns and inns—all these were potential sites for instruction. One day he found Demosthenes having a meal at a tavern. On seeing Diogenes, the orator retreated to the rear in order to avoid being accosted. At this the philosopher smiled and called after him, "The further you draw back, the more you'll be sucked in."[34]

Diogenes's concentration on the events of daily life may suggest that he had no interest whatever in intellectual pursuits. Quite the contrary.

Diogenes, Author and Intellectual

Diogenes was a prolific author, if the list of works traditionally attributed to him can be credited. The role these writings played in disseminating his thought is impossible to determine, however.

Doubt has been cast on the authenticity of the works ascribed to Diogenes since antiquity; Sosicrates of Rhodes and Satyrus the Peripatetic claimed that he left nothing behind in writing.[35] Making Diogenes a clone of Socrates would nonetheless be a mistake. For the Cynics did write. Antisthenes composed a large number of works, which Diogenes Laertius listed in ten volumes.[36] Among Diogenes's disciples, Monimus wrote poetry as well as two books, *On Impulses* and an *Exhortation to Philosophy*; Onesicritus composed a book on the education of Alexander the Great, the *Alexandropaedia*; Crates wrote tragedies in addition to a volume of letters.[37] And Crates's pupil Metrocles produced a series of works that ultimately he chose to burn.[38]

Diogenes Laertius transmitted two lists of Diogenes's works. The first, established by an unidentified source, contained the titles of thirteen treatises and seven tragedies, and a volume of letters. The second, attributed to Sotion, a grammarian from Alexandria active in the third and second centuries BCE, seems to have been the result of an attempt to separate genuine works from spurious ones; it contains a dozen titles in no particular order, a volume of *chreiai* (anecdotes probably collected by another scholar), and a volume of letters.[39]

Apart from the letters, very probably apocryphal, the two lists have only four titles in common: *Pardalis, Cephalion, On Love,* and *Aristarchus.* The second list was very probably due to an athetesis that rejected all those works found to be incompatible with Stoic tradition.[40] This partisan exercise in expurgation was probably responsible for the absence, in Sotion's list, of the *Republic,* a work that has long been firmly attributed to Diogenes. It would also explain the absence of the tragedies, which, relying on mythical accounts, treated topics that the Stoics considered to be extremely indelicate, such as cannibalism (*Thyestes*) and incest and parricide (*Oedipus*). Certain ancient thinkers, including even some Cynics, had a low opinion of the tragedies. Julian, for example, felt sure they could not have come from Diogenes's hand. "What reader of these would not abhor them," he asked, "and find in them an excess of infamy not to be surpassed even by courtesans?"[41]

Accordingly, these works were often ascribed to one or another of Diogenes's disciples—Philiscus of Aegina, for example, or Pasiphon.[42] And yet in the *Suda* one finds Diogenes mentioned as the author of eight tragedies. Of these, seven figure in the first list of Diogenes's works. Diogenes himself hinted at the usefulness of tragedy as a literary form, for it allowed him to treat themes that were at the heart of his philosophy: "All the things of which tragedies speak are to be found in me: I am 'poor, condemned to wander, living from hand to mouth.' But whatever my condition, I am ready to do battle—even against the king of Persia—for the sake of happiness."[43]

If Diogenes was in fact able to devote himself to writing, as there is good reason to believe, his material circumstances must have differed, at least intermittently, from the ones described by our sources. He must have had a table, writing materials, and a place protected against the elements where he could work and store his scrolls. Parchment was expensive, so he would have been obliged to economize by writing on both sides, as Lucian pointed out.[44] Moreover, Diogenes is said to have possessed a personal library, also to have shared his manuscripts with others.[45] Since we know that he did not hesitate to ask for assistance, it may be that certain people of his acquaintance offered to help him, discreetly furnishing the materials and working space he needed in order to compose his written works.

Tragedies, in the classical period, were meant not to be read, but to be performed as part of the dramatic festival held every year in honor of Dionysus. It seems likely, then, that Diogenes took part in the competition for best tragedy, and therefore that he sought glory more than he cared to admit. Diogenes Laertius says that he called the performances at the Dionysia "a spectacle for morons."[46] And yet, in fourth-century Athens, there was no more powerful medium than theater. Animated by an unshakable determination to educate his contemporaries, Diogenes was not averse to attending banquets or sporting events; for the very same reason, he might well have resolved to take part in the life of the theater, not only as a spectator, but also as an author.

In addition to philosophical writings and poetic compositions, Diogenes regularly distinguished himself, in the anecdotes known to us, by his knowledge of literature. This knowledge did not seem incompatible, in the eyes of those who related these anecdotes, with the basic thrust of Cynicism. Diogenes quoted famous authors and adapted passages from tragic works and verses of epic (particularly Homeric) poetry for his own purposes. Thus, for example, in turning away a pupil whom he considered unsuited to philosophy, he recalled the line in the *Iliad* where Zeus says to his son Ares, wounded by Diomedes, "Do not sit beside me and whine, you double-faced liar."[47] On another occasion, "breakfasting on olives embedded in a flat cake, he tossed the cake away and said, 'Stranger, get out of the tyrants' way'"—echoing Laius, ordering Oedipus to let him pass, in Euripides's *Phoenician Women*.[48]

Diogenes therefore knew his classics. Nevertheless, he was of two minds about the value of learning. On the one hand, he looked favorably upon education (*paideia*), which he considered beneficial to persons of all ages: "For the young an instiller of temperance [*sophrosynē*], for the elderly a consolation [*paramuthia*], for the poor a richness [*ploutos*], and for the rich an ornament [*kosmos*]."[49] On the other hand, he held that certain disciplines of the traditional curriculum were of no interest; according to his biographer, he "neglected music, geometry, astrology, and other such studies, judging them useless and unnecessary."[50]

Diogenes's Political Philosophy

Just as he joined in the spirit of his time by writing a treatise (now lost) on economics, so too he turned his attention to political philosophy, another popular topic of the fourth century. In this he was preceded by Plato and, a few decades later, Aristotle.

The attribution of a *Politeia* to Diogenes is not entirely secure; some commentators have argued that a forger composed the work with the aim of discrediting the philosopher and his school. And yet the history of its transmission does not seem to support the charge of inauthenticity. The main part of what survives has come down to us from Philodemus of Gadara, an Epicurean, who composed a treatise in the first century BCE on the Stoics in

which he discusses Diogenes's *Republic*. Moreover, the evidence
he marshals in favor of the attribution of the treatise to Diogenes
is persuasive. The work was listed under Diogenes's name in the
catalogues and libraries of the period. Philodemus also points
out that several authors, slightly later than Diogenes, sanctioned
this attribution: Cleanthes of Assos, in the third century; his contemporary Chrysippus of Soli; and, in the century following,
Antipater of Tarsus. All three were Stoics who would have had
a motive for purging the Cynic corpus of this work. Philodemus
himself, unsurprisingly, considering his lack of sympathy for the
argument developed in the *Republic*, emphasizes only its most
subversive aspects.

Quite a few, but not all, of the ideas found in the fragments that
have been preserved are of Cynic inspiration, among them the futility
of armed warfare and the corresponding need for it to be banned;
the elimination of coinage and its replacement by knucklebones,
which is to say a purely fiduciary currency; the abolition of private
property, also of the family and familial bonds; the authorization of
incest and parricide; approval of indiscriminate sexual relations, of
sexual freedom for women, and of joint ownership of assets with
men by women and children; an end to social distinctions between
men and women, so that they would be permitted to wear the same
clothes and pursue the same activities in the same places (stadiums
and palaestrae, for example); finally, acceptance (though not en-
couragement) of cannibalism.

Contrary to what one might expect, however, there is nothing
in Diogenes's *Republic* that argues against citizenship or a government of laws as a matter of principle. Indeed, according to Diogenes
Laertius, Diogenes stressed the importance of law in a memorable
syllogism:

> Without the city there is no means of obtaining the advantages of
> civilized life. The city is a civilized thing; its advantages cannot be
> enjoyed without law; and therefore law is a civilized thing.[51]

In working out the implications of this line of reasoning, Diogenes indicted all those who posed a threat to cities and their laws, foremost among them tyrants and demagogues.

Tyrants and Demagogues

On being asked by an unknown tyrant what bronze was best for a statue, Diogenes is said to have replied, "The kind from which Harmodius and Aristogeiton were forged."[52] These two men had been put to death for having assassinated the Athenian tyrant Hipparchus in 514. Revered afterward as heroes of democracy, they were memorialized by the statues in the Agora that Diogenes alludes to here. His sympathy for tyrannicide reflected the prevailing opinion in democratic circles of the period. In Athens, the so-called law of Eucrates, dating from 337–336, guaranteed that no one who killed a tyrant or anyone who had threatened to destroy democracy would suffer any dishonor of the sort attaching to an ordinary murderer. A few years earlier, an anti-tyrant law in the city of Eretria granted a long series of privileges to anyone who killed a tyrant or an aspirant to tyranny.

Asked about the manner in which the tyrant Dionysius of Syracuse (who reigned in that city during the first third of the fourth century) treated his friends, Diogenes replied, "Like sacks: when they're full he hangs them up, when empty he discards them."[53] More generally, he pointed to the characteristic failings of tyrants: their disloyalty, their egotism, their need to manipulate others. On this subject, as on many others, Diogenes placed himself in opposition to Plato, who had traveled to the court of Dionysius in Syracuse, and later to that of his son, Dionysius the Younger, with the avowed intention of converting them to the practice of good government. It is possible that Diogenes met Dionysius II in Corinth, at the end of his tyranny, in 343. What Diogenes objected to was not Plato's own trenchant criticism of tyrants, but his willingness to consort with them. Diogenes Laertius reports a sharp exchange between the two men. Seeing Diogenes washing some lettuces, Plato said to him, "If you [had] courted Dionysius, you wouldn't be washing lettuces." To this Diogenes calmly answered, "And if you [had] washed lettuces, you wouldn't have courted Dionysius."[54]

Diogenes also regularly attacked another enemy of democracy—populists, known as demagogues because they flattered the people by telling them what they wanted to hear. But he went further, holding that all politicians were liable to succumb to the same temptation. It was for this reason that he had particular admiration for those who considered taking up a political career and then decided against it. He called demagogues *diakonoi ochlou*—servants of the mob, valets of the rabble. The use of the term *ochlos*, which designated the irrational crowd, shows that Diogenes mistrusted ordinary people every bit as much as he did demagogues, and regarded ochlocracy, government by an inconstant and unreasoning populace, as a great evil. Diogenes and Plato agreed on this point at least, that only philosophers were qualified to govern cities. But unlike Plato, Diogenes not only refused to become a counselor to princes, but also attached great importance to educating the masses.

Diogenes routinely drew attention to the dysfunctional aspects of politics and the evils of democracy. But so far as we can tell, he did not treat in any real detail a question that, in the minds of Greek citizens, was no less fundamental, namely, the place of religion in civic life.

Diogenes and the Gods

Religion seems not to have been a subject of great concern for Diogenes. In this he departed from the example of his mentor, Antisthenes, the only one of the Cynics who displayed a sustained interest in theological questions. The fragments of the *Republic* that have come down to us make no mention of the gods in relation to human affairs. Similarly, among the titles of the treatises attributed to Diogenes, none bears upon a religious topic.

With regard to such matters Diogenes was heir to a venerable skeptical tendency that extended well beyond the Cynic school. Philosophers had questioned various elements of ritual practice as early as the sixth century. In the fifth, some went so far as to question the existence of the gods. Protagoras, in his essay *On the Gods*, staked out an agnostic position, famously stated by its opening sentence: "As for the gods, I cannot know either that they exist or that they do not exist."[55] Prodicus of Ceos argued that, as a consequence of observing nature, those things of the physical world on which human existence depends—the sun, moon, rivers, and so on—were transformed into divinities.[56] Critias, in a surviving fragment of his satirical play *Sisyphus*, maintained that the gods were a product of a wise man's desire to instill fear in human beings and in this way help to limit their misdeeds.[57]

Unlike Plato, Aristotle, and members of the Stoic school, Diogenes and his followers showed little interest in theological speculation. The principal Cynic claim in this connection was that religion was not a fact of nature, but a custom, a human convention, and for that reason constituted an obstacle to self-sufficiency, happiness, and liberty. Animals were superior to human beings because they had no conception of divinity and therefore could enjoy a life free from anxiety. But this position did not amount to impiety: while relativizing the form that men gave to their beliefs, it did not contest their soundness.

If Diogenes had little to say about religion in general, he nonetheless sharply criticized ritual practices, pointing out their incoherence, the naivete they exploited among the faithful, and the utilitarian orientation of the various cults. He scolded those who made sacrifices in the hope of being favored by good health, only then to gorge themselves on food and drink once the ceremony was over. The trust that believers placed in these rites astonished him: seeing someone perform a ritual purification, he asked, "Don't you realize that by sprinkling yourself you can no more correct your mistakes in life than your errors in grammar?"[58]

Diogenes denounced the obsession with prayers, offerings, and sacrifices, which often were misguided and seldom led to anything good. "When some parents were sacrificing in the hope that a son might be born to them," Diogenes Laertius relates, "he asked, 'But shouldn't you be more concerned with what sort of man he will turn out to be?'"[59] He scoffed at those who believed they had obtained advantages in the next world, superior even to those of the most virtuous statesmen and military figures of their time, simply because they had been initiated in the Mysteries. To those who encouraged him to undergo initiation in order to receive special treatment in Hades, Diogenes responded, "It would be laughable if [the famous war heroes] Agesilaus and Epaminondas live in the mire, while nobodies inhabit the Isles of the Blessed because they've been initiated."[60]

The folly of those who listened to soothsayers and interpreters of dreams he found no less absurd. According to Diogenes Laertius, "He used to say that when he saw pilots, physicians, and philosophers at their work he regarded man as the wisest of all animals; but when he observed dream interpreters, prophets, and those who listen to them, ... he found no creature more foolish."[61] He ridiculed the magical phrases that some people wrote down on the walls of their homes in a futile attempt to ward off evil. Institutional religion he thought corrupt. One day he witnessed temple magistrates arrest a steward who had stolen a votive bowl. "The big thieves," he observed, "are leading away the little one."[62]

The nature of Diogenes's religious beliefs has given rise to considerable debate among historians of philosophy. Some consider him to have been atheist, others pantheist, still others agnostic. The last of these three characterizations probably comes closest to the truth. For Diogenes, the gods fulfilled several purposes. They allowed him to hold up self-sufficiency as an ideal toward which all human beings must strive; to stress the need to persevere in the face of the ordeals that earthly existence holds in store for them; and also to emphasize that nature is something that human beings must come to terms with, because it cannot be evaded or overcome. The gods functioned, in other words, as a useful fiction. In this connection Diogenes frequently mentioned Tyche, the goddess of fortune, whose cult had become increasingly popular in Greek cities of the early fourth century. The trials and tribulations of human life, personified by Tyche, could be resisted only by means of mockery and disdain.

With regard to theology, Diogenes seems to have agreed with Protagoras that the existence of the gods could be neither proved nor disproved. The Carthaginian theologian Tertullian reports that when Diogenes was asked what was taking place in heaven, he answered by saying, "I have never been up there." At the same time Diogenes felt that people behaved better when they lived in fear of being punished, and for this reason credited religious belief with a certain social utility. Asked whether the gods actually existed, he replied, "I do not know, only that they ought to exist."[63]

Religious belief made it more difficult for human beings to achieve self-sufficiency, however, and therefore was not absolutely desirable. But since neither Diogenes nor his disciples considered theology to be a subject of any great philosophical import, we know nothing more about their teaching in this regard.

The Cynic School

By virtue of his status as a foreigner, Diogenes was unable to take part in political life. Nevertheless, he exerted a considerable influence on intellectual life through his pupils, who preserved, developed, and spread his ideas in the centuries following his death. Diogenes Laertius discusses a number of them in the sixth book of his *Lives of the Eminent Philosophers*. Among Diogenes's own disciples were Monimus of Syracuse, Onesicritus of Astypalaea, and

Crates of Thebes; among those of Crates were Hipparchia and her brother, Metrocles of Maroneia (initially a pupil of the Peripatetic philosopher Theophrastus).

Diogenes had sufficiently many students to be perceived by his contemporaries as a teacher; indeed, people asked him to educate their children. In most cities, because the cost of instruction was borne by the parents, tuition was reserved for the children of elite families. The social profile of Diogenes's pupils was much more varied, however, ranging from Monimus, the manservant of a Corinthian banker, to Crates, a very wealthy Theban who, on deciding to devote his life to philosophy, gave away a fortune of some two hundred talents to his fellow citizens.

The passion for philosophy that Diogenes inspired in his students suggests he must have been uncommonly charismatic, though our written sources provide little evidence of this. Still, he was capable of captivating entire families: when Androsthenes of Aegina began attending Diogenes's lectures, he was subsequently joined by his older brother, Philiscus, and then by their father, Onesicritus.[64] But unlike many professors of rhetoric, who welcomed anyone who could afford their fee, Diogenes selected his students on the basis of tests of character. To one candidate he handed a small salted fish and told him to follow him; ashamed, the young man threw away the fish and rushed off. In another version of the same episode, Diogenes gave a small cheese to the applicant.[65] These two foods, cheese and fish, consumed in meager amounts, were emblems of the Cynic mendicant's daily diet. Refusing to carry them for fear of being taken for a beggar, or for a servant carrying his master's meals, at once disqualified anyone aspiring to the Cynic way of life.

Diogenes's selective method of recruitment stood the usual teacher-student relationship in the Greek educational marketplace on its head. He rejected those he thought unworthy of his lessons, particularly the gilded youth of Athens who flocked to the lectures of the Sophists. But still more than their students, Diogenes rejected the teaching of the Sophists themselves. They had first appeared in the second half of the fifth century, living on the income from their fees and, for the most part, leading an itinerant life. The majority of those who stayed in Athens came from elsewhere: Gorgias came from Leontinoi, Protagoras from Abdera, Prodicus from Ceos, Hippias from Elis, Thrasymachus from Chalcedon. In the *Protagoras*, Plato described the Sophist as "a master of making one a clever speaker."[66] But the expertise of some of those who were called Sophists went well beyond a mastery of rhetoric; Hippias, for example, was reputed to be a man of encyclopedic learning and a master of all the technical arts. The instruction given by the Sophists was expensive, and Socrates reproached them for taking anyone as a student so long as he could pay what they charged.

With time their faults became magnified in the eyes of ordinary people, who resented the fact that, as foreigners, they earned a very good living by teaching young people from wealthy families how to manipulate the masses. They were frequently criticized, sometimes with grave consequences. Protagoras, brought to trial on a charge of impiety, was expelled from Athens; copies of his books in private hands were confiscated and burned in the Agora, the very place where Diogenes was to lay his head a few decades later. Diogenes was spared such a fate, probably because he did not seek to profit from the aspiration of Athenian elites to control the city's destiny, any more than he cared about pleasing the powerful.

Diogenes and Alexander

Diogenes is said to have met a number of the great figures of his age, not only Philip II, king of Macedonia, and his son Alexander, but also Craterus and Antipater, officers of the Macedonian army who became famous for having triumphed over the Athenians and their allies at the Battle of Crannon in 322. The best documented of all these encounters is the one with Alexander. Dio Chrysostom devoted an entire discourse to it, *On Kingship*.[67] The historical veracity of this episode has long been contested. And yet, as we saw earlier, there is no reason a priori to dismiss its possibility. The paths of the two men might have crossed on several occasions, in Chaeronea, Athens, and Corinth. It was in Corinth that the account that has come down to us is situated, more precisely outside the city in the Craneion, a hillside known in antiquity for its cypress grove and gymnasium, where Diogenes is supposed to have made his home.[68]

Alexander went to Corinth at the beginning of 336, a few months after the assassination of his father and his own elevation to the Macedonian throne, with the aim of strengthening the diplomatic ties established by Philip II with the Greek city-states and extinguishing any desire for independence on their part. A few months later he set off to the north, crossing the Danube, but before long was forced to come back to Greece to suppress an uprising by Theban democrats provoked by rumors of his death.

At some point in the second half of 336, Alexander passed through Athens on his way to Corinth. In a famous passage, Plutarch reports his arrival there:

The Greeks held a general assembly at the Isthmus and voted to embark on an expedition against the Persians with Alexander, who was proclaimed as their leader. Many statesmen and philosophers came to congratulate him, and he hoped that Diogenes of Sinope, who was living in Corinth, would do likewise; but since he paid not the slightest heed to Alexander, but remained at his leisure in the Craneion, Alexander himself went to see him and found him stretched out in the sun. At the approach of so many people, Diogenes sat up a little and fixed his eyes on Alexander. And when the king greeted him and asked him if there was anything that he wanted, he said, "Yes, that you should stand a little out of my sun." It is said that Alexander was so impressed by this, and by the arrogance and grandeur of spirit of a man who could treat him with such disdain, that he said to his courtiers, who were laughing and joking about the philosopher as they were walking away, "But I'll tell you this, if I were not Alexander, I would be Diogenes!"[69]

The interest of philosophers in Alexander is well known, and not only on account of this extraordinary interview. Aristotle had tutored him in his youth. Crates conversed with him before he razed Crates's native city of Thebes in 335.[70] Onesicritus, another one of Diogenes's disciples, accompanied Alexander on his campaigns and composed a treatise, now lost, on the education of the Macedonian king.[71] The idea that Alexander might have met Diogenes is by no means implausible, then, and all the less as Diogenes's presence in Athens and Corinth in 336 is relatively well established.

During the summer and fall of that year the lives of three of the most famous men of the 330s were to intersect more than once. The third one, alongside Alexander and Diogenes, we have already encountered: Dioxippus of Athens, who triumphed in the pankration competition at the Olympic games in 336 and subsequently accompanied Alexander on his campaigns. Though forgotten today, he was famous in the Greek world also for his victory, in the presence of the king, over the Macedonian soldier Coragus. The many ancient accounts of this combat relate that Dioxippus, his naked body oiled, wearing a helmet and armed only with a heavy club, managed in a few seconds to wrestle Coragus to the ground and disable him, even though Coragus was equipped, in Macedonian fashion, with a javelin, a long pike, and a sword.[72] Things ended badly for the great athlete, however. The Macedonians took their revenge by conspiring to make it appear that he had stolen a golden cup, as a result of which, depending on the account, Dioxippus was executed or committed suicide.

Diogenes had gone to Olympia in July 336 and saw Dioxippus claim victory unopposed. A few weeks later Diogenes went to Athens to witness the champion's triumphal entry into the city, and then continued on to Corinth to enjoy the last days of summer.

There he may well have met Alexander, who had previously gone through Athens on his return from Macedonia.

The destinies of the two men are bound together in ancient tradition, so much so that they were supposed to have died on the same day, Alexander in Babylon and Diogenes in Greece.[73] This taste for synchronicity, pronounced among Greek historians of the period, gave rise to the belief, for example, that the naval battle between Greek and Persian forces at Salamis, in the Saronic Gulf southwest of Athens, took place on the same day in September 480 as the infantry battle between Greek and Carthaginian forces at Himera, a Greek city in northwest Sicily.

The presumptive coincidence of the deaths of Diogenes and Alexander constitutes above all an extension and an echo of their meeting. But the probability that the two most famous men of their time died on the same day is small. The date of Alexander's death is well established: during the night of June 10–11, 323. By comparison, the very place where Diogenes died is a matter of dispute: in Corinth, either in the Craneion or in the house of his former master Xeniades; or in Athens, where he is said to have asked that his body be thrown into the Ilissus; or perhaps near Olympia.[74]

Dying a Philosopher's Death

On the circumstances of Diogenes's death, our sources disagree. Ancient tradition accommodates four main versions. According to the first, Diogenes died of complications from eating a raw octopus in an attempt to demonstrate the uselessness of cooking.[75] If so, this would not have been the first time he had conducted such an experiment; Diogenes Laertius recalls that he once suffered indigestion from eating raw meat.[76] A second tradition, due to the Cynic philosopher Cercidas of Megalopolis and accepted by members of certain other schools, holds that he deliberately asphyxiated himself beneath his cloak and was found lifeless in the gymnasium in the

Craneion.[77] A third view is that he was bitten while trying to divide an octopus among some dogs and died of the infection this caused.[78] Diogenes Laertius himself composed an epigram in support of this version:

A: Diogenes, tell us what fate took you to Hades.
D: A dog's savage tooth.[79]

The fourth opinion is that he died after coming down with a fever while traveling to the Olympic games.[80]

There was a tendency in ancient Greece and Rome to see the circumstances under which philosophers died as constituting a final affirmation or, conversely, a cruel repudiation of their teaching.[81] In the case of Diogenes, the reports of his death are remarkable for their inventiveness, causing it to be an object of debate no less intense than the controversy surrounding the philosopher's indifference to the fate reserved for his mortal remains. Diogenes's own view, well summarized by Teles, was shared by all the Cynics that came after him:

What difference is there between being consumed by fire, devoured by a dog, left above ground to be preyed upon by vultures, or buried below ground to be eaten by worms?[82]

Diogenes Underground

Diogenes is said to have made it clear that he did not wish to be buried in a proper grave. Here again there are several rival versions. Some say he asked that his corpse be abandoned to every manner of wild beast; according to others, that it be thrown into a pit and covered with dirt, but not so much that it could not be eaten by dogs, his brothers; or that it be left out in the open, exposed to the sun and the rain; still others say he directed that it be thrown into the Ilissus.[83]

Cicero reports a conversation in which Diogenes contemplated his demise:

> Diogenes was a rougher character [than Socrates], and although he held the same views on this matter, he expressed it more brutally in the Cynic fashion, ordering that he should be thrown out unburied. When his friends exclaimed, "What, to fall prey to birds and beasts?," he replied, "Not at all, you must lay my stick down beside me to enable me to drive them away." "But how will you be able to do that," they said, "since you will no longer be conscious?" "Well, if I'm not aware of anything, how can it harm me to be ripped apart by wild beasts?"[84]

Nevertheless, Diogenes's final wishes seem not to have been respected. A tradition reported by Diogenes Laertius has it that the question of who would bury the Cynic in Corinth provoked a violent quarrel among his disciples, settled finally when the magistrates and leading citizens of the city authorized his interment beside the gate opening onto the Isthmus.[85] Eubulus, for his part, says that he was buried by Xeniades's children, whose tutor he had been.[86]

Pausanias, writing in the second century CE, noted that among the tombs visible to the traveler approaching Corinth was that of Diogenes.[87] Neither the funerary monument he mentions nor the inscription it ought to have borne has been found, giving free rein to the imagination of poets. Under Augustus, Antipater of Thessalonica composed the following epitaph:

> This is the tomb of Diogenes, the wise Cynic, who once with manly spirit practised an ascetic life; who had one wallet, one cloak, one staff to accompany his steps, the armor of self-sufficient moderation. Immoderate fools, keep clear of this tomb; even in Hades the Sinopean hates all men who are base.[88]

Many authors celebrated Diogenes's memory post mortem, beginning with his disciple Philiscus of Aegina, whose epigram, engraved on the base of the statue erected in the Cynic's hometown in modern times, I quoted at the outset of the present work. Visitors to the Museo Maffeiano in Verona are able to read another epigram, set on four lines and engraved on a white marble stele (Fig. 14):

> Tell me, dog, over the grave of what man are you standing guard?
> "Of the Dog." But who is this man who is the Dog?" "Diogenes."
> What is his ancestry? "Sinopean." The one who lived in a *pithos*?
> "Indeed; but now having died, he has his home among the stars."

But they mustn't be taken in. The stele in question, which formerly was part of the epigraphic collection of the Palazzo Miniscalchi-Erizzo, was not found in Corinth. It is a modern fake, made on the basis of the text transmitted by two collections of ancient epigrams, the *Palatine Anthology* and the *Planudean Anthology*. By contrast, an authentic but very incomplete inscription from the imperial period has been found in Sinope, having to do with a philosopher whose name ends in *-ogénē* and who was honored by the inhabitants of Themiscyrus; it may have been engraved on a monument in honor of Diogenes.

In view of the presence of a tomb at Corinth, combined with the account of Diogenes's death in the Craneion and with the possible involvement of local officials in approving his burial, it is tempting to conclude that he died on the Isthmus. As for the exact circumstances of his passing, no doubt Diogenes carried them away with him. The versions that mention the eating of an octopus, the dispute with a dog, and self-inflicted asphyxiation seem like so many philosophical constructions, too good to be true. The likeliest explanation is that Diogenes died of old age, perhaps during his last summer in Corinth, in 323 or thereabouts.

His arrival in the underworld was a source of poetic inspiration. Two of the most memorable texts that have come down to us are by Leonidas of Tarentum and Honestus of Corinth. The first, composed in the third century BCE, imagines Diogenes addressing Charon, the ferryman of the dead:

> Mournful minister of Hades, who traverse this water of Acheron in your dark boat, receive me, Diogenes the Dog, even though your gruesome bark is overloaded with spirits of the dead. My luggage is but a flask, and a wallet, and my old cloak, and the obol that pays the passage of the departed. All that was mine in life I bring with me to Hades, and have nothing left beneath the sun.[89]

Honestus, writing under Augustus, imagined Diogenes talking to the dog of Hades, Cerberus, playing on the Cynic's familiarity with this animal:

> The staff, and wallet, and thick cloak were the very light burden of wise Diogenes in life. ["]I bring all to the ferryman, for I left nothing on earth. But you, Cerberus dog, fawn on me, the Dog.["][90]

"Dog" for Leonidas, "wise man" for Honestus, "wise dog" for Antipater, "heavenly dog" for Cercidas, "authentic dog" for Julian, "the man from Sinope" for Lucian, "Socrates gone mad" for Plato— Diogenes was loaded down with epithets by the ancients. But the moderns were not to be outdone. He has been called a "wise tramp," a "demoniacal sage," a "hirsute hermit"; Nietzsche called him a "shameless buffoon" and a "scholarly satyr"; Roger-Pol Droit called him a "Heracles of consistency."

Aelius Theon, an Alexandrian Sophist of the first century CE, reported that, in response to someone who asked him how to become famous, he said, "Concern yourself as little as possible with becoming famous."[91] In Diogenes's case, this way of acting could not have been more successful.

NOTES

Introduction

1. Philiscus of Aegina, *Greek Anthology* 16.334, trans. W. R. Paton (Cambridge, MA: Harvard University Press, 1918). [Authorship of this epigram is assigned by Paton to Antiphilus of Byzantium, an attribution that has been revised by subsequent scholarship; Paton's rendering here has been slightly modified. —Trans.]

2. On the transformation of the Greek "jar" (*pithos*) into the Latin "barrel" (*dolium*), see the author's explanation in Chapter 2. —Trans.

3. The French contains an untranslatable rhyme: *lanterne* (lantern or lamp) at the end of the first line is echoed by the homophonic phrase *lent terne* (slow lifeless) at the end of the third. —Trans.

4. Here and throughout I use the terms "mendicancy" and "mendicant" synonymously with "begging" and "beggar," not in the sense of soliciting charitable donations, as in the Christian tradition of almsgiving, but in the specifically Greek sense of *apaitein*, which is to say asking for what one is rightfully owed. Thus Diogenes considered himself entitled to a basic level of subsistence in exchange for the teaching he dispensed. See, for example, Diogenes Laertius 6.46. —Trans.

5. Diogenes Laertius, *Lives of the Eminent Philosophers* 6.103, trans. Pamela Mensch, ed. James Miller (New York: Oxford University Press, 2020); see also 1.18–20. [Unless otherwise indicated, all translations from Diogenes Laertius refer to the Oxford edition. Readers may also wish to consult Stephen White's recent and still more extensively annotated translation (New York: Cambridge University Press, 2021). —Trans.]

6. Cicero, *On Duties*, trans. Walter Miller (Cambridge, MA: Harvard University Press, 1913), 1.148.

Chapter 1

1. See the introduction to M.-O. Goulet-Cazé, *Diogène Laërce: Vies et doctrines des philosophes illustres*, 2nd ed. (Paris: Le Livre de Poche, 1999).

2. See D. Gutas, "Sayings by Diogenes Preserved in Arabic," in R. Goulet and M.-O. Goulet-Cazé, eds., *Le Cynisme ancien et ses prolongements* (Paris: Presses Universitaires de France, 1993), 475–518.

3. See M. Onfray, "Le nouveau Diogènes est arrivé," foreword to A. Baldacchino, *Diogènes le Cynique: Fragments inédits* (Paris: Éditions Autrement, 2013), 17.

4. See Diogenes Laertius 6.38, 6.43.

5. See Seneca, *De Consolatione ad Helviam* 11.7.2, and Pliny, *Natural History* 5.112.

6. The phrase *paracharattein to nomisma* (restamp the currency) signifies the counterfeiting of coins or the adulteration of money. See L. E. Navia, *Diogenes the Cynic: The War Against the World* (Amherst, NY: Humanity Books, 2005), 226; also Mensch's note at Diogenes Laertius 198n29. The oracle's phrase bears a double meaning: *nomisma* may refer not only to coinage but also to social customs, so restamping in this case can mean to alter social norms. On the related reference to *politikon nomisma*, see Roubineau's discussion below. —Trans.

7. See Diogenes Laertius 6.20–21.

8. See Diogenes Laertius 6.20.

9. See Plato, *Apology* 20c–24e.

10. See Diogenes Laertius 7.2.

11. See Diogenes Laertius 6.21.

12. See Aristotle, *Politics* 1259a.

13. See Isocrates, *Antidosis* 155.

14. See Diogenes Laertius 4.46.

15. See Plutarch, *Moralia* 294 [= *On Tranquillity of Mind* 19.6].

16. Favorinus, *On Exile* 4.2; quoted in Léonce Paquet, *Les Cyniques grecs: Fragments et témoignages*, 2nd ed. (Ottawa: Les Presses de l'Université d'Ottawa, 1988), 80.

17. Antipater, *Greek Anthology* 11.158, trans. W. R. Paton (Cambridge, MA: Harvard University Press, 1918). [Paton's version slightly modified. —Trans.]

18. See Dio Chrysostom, *Discourses* 1.84, 4.32, 8.28, 8.30.

19. Thus the famous exchange reported by Diogenes Laertius (6.49): "When . . . someone remarked, 'The Sinopeans sentenced you to exile,' [Diogenes] replied, 'And I sentenced *them* to stay at home.'" —Trans.

20. See Euripides, *Phoenician Women* 1449–1450.

21. Fragmenta Adespota 281, in A. Nauck, ed., *Tragicorum Graecorum Fragmenta*, 2nd ed. (Leipzig: Teubner, 1889); quoted in Paquet, *Les Cyniques grecs*, 151.

22. Diogenes Laertius 6.10.

23. Diogenes Laertius 6.43.

24. See Aelian, *Historical Miscellany* 12.58.

25. Dio Chrysostom, *Discourses* 9.1 [= *Isthmian Discourse*], quoted in Paquet, *Les Cyniques grecs*, 203.

26. See Dio Chrysostom, *Discourses* 8.12 [= *Diogenes, or On Virtue*].

27. See Dio Chrysostom, *Discourses* 9.10.

28. See Lucian, *Herodotus, or Aëtion* 1.

29. See Diogenes Laertius 6.2.

30. See Lucian, *Passing of Peregrinus* 1–2.

31. Aelian, *Historical Miscellany* 9.28, trans. N. G. Wilson (Cambridge, MA: Harvard University Press, 1997).

32. Johannes Stobaeus, *Florilegium*, ms. M, 13.25; quoted in Paquet, *Les Cyniques grecs*, 94. [Cf. another version of this story, also recorded by Stobaeus (3.13.43), where Diogenes replies, "But a physician, because he is responsible for restoring people to good health, does not minister to those who are healthy." —Trans.]

33. Dio Chrysostom, *Discourses* 8.5; quoted in Paquet, *Les Cyniques grecs*, 196.

34. Here I paraphrase the French actor and director Sacha Guitry (1885–1957).

35. See Stobaeus, *Florilegium*, ms. M, 45.28.

36. See M. Cambron-Goulet, "Les Cyniques, penseurs dans la norme et citoyens de la marge," *Cahiers des Études Anciennes* 44 (2007): 109–136.

37. Fragmenta Adespota 536, in Nauck, *Tragicorum Graecorum Fragmenta*; quoted in Paquet, *Les Cyniques grecs*, 150.

38. Diogenes Laertius 6.63, 6.72.

39. Lucian, *The Cynic* 15; in *The Cynic Philosophers: From Diogenes to Julian*, ed. and trans. R. Dobbin (New York: Penguin, 2012).

40. Diogenes Laertius 6.98.

41. This according to Seneca, *On Benefits* 7.1.7; quoted in Paquet, *Les Cyniques grecs*, 225.

42. See Favorinus, *On Exile* 10.1.

Chapter 2

1. Anon., *Greek Anthology* 9.145, trans. W. R. Paton (Cambridge, MA: Harvard University Press, 1917).

2. Diogenes Laertius 6.50.

3. See Plutarch, *Alexander* 14.

4. This account is due to Dionysius the Stoic; see Diogenes Laertius 6.43.

5. Diogenes Laertius 6.41.

6. See Philo, *Every Good Man Is Free* 157.

7. Diogenes Laertius 6.75.

8. Johannes Stobaeus, *Florilegium*, ms. M, 97.31; quoted in Léonce Paquet, *Les Cyniques grecs: Fragments et témoignages*, 2nd ed. (Ottawa: Les Presses de l'Université d'Ottawa, 1988), 156.

9. See Raymond Descat, "Aux origines de l'oikonomia' grecque," *Quaderni Urbinati di Cultura Classica* 28, no. 1 (1988): 103–119.

10. *Gnomologium Vaticanum* 169; quoted in Paquet, *Les Cyniques grecs*, 67.

11. Diogenes Laertius 6.74.

12. Diogenes Laertius 6.104. [In the second part of this passage I follow the French text in preference to Mensch. —Trans.]

13. *Gnomologium Vaticanum* 182; quoted in Paquet, *Les Cyniques grecs*, 76. [An obol was worth one-sixth of a drachma, roughly what a skilled worker could expect to earn in a day; see *Diogenes the Cynic: Sayings and Anecdotes*, trans. R. Hard (Oxford: Oxford University Press, 2012), 184n16. —Trans.]

14. Xenophon, *Oeconomicus* 2.4, trans. E. C. Marchant, revised by J. Henderson (Cambridge, MA: Harvard University Press, 2013). [Henderson's revision slightly modified. —Trans.]

15. See Xenophon, *Symposium* 3.8, trans. O. J. Todd, revised by J. Henderson (Cambridge, MA: Harvard University Press, 2013). [The reference is to the handful or so of sandy soil that a wrestler sprinkled over his body after oiling it. —Trans.]

16. See Pierre Bourdieu, *La misère du monde* (Paris: Seuil, 1993).

17. Stobaeus, *Florilegium*, ms. M, 97.31; quoted in Paquet, *Les Cyniques grecs*, 155.

18. Stobaeus, *Florilegium*, ms. M, 10.63; quoted in Paquet, *Les Cyniques grecs*, 92.

19. Plutarch, *Table Talk* 2.1.7 [= 632e], trans. P. A. Clement (Cambridge, MA: Harvard University Press, 1969). [Clement's version slightly modified. —Trans.]

20. See Diogenes Laertius 6.57.

21. Antiphilus of Byzantium, *Greek Anthology* 16.333, trans. W. R. Paton (Cambridge, MA: Harvard University Press, 1918).

22. Artemidorus, *Oneirocritica* 3.53.

23. See *Corpus Paroemiographorum Graecorum* 2.15.7.

24. Aelian, *Historical Miscellany* 13.26; *Diogenes the Cynic*, trans. Hard, 9, no. 9b.

25. Xenophon, *Symposium* 4.43.

26. Diogenes Laertius 6.23.

27. On the Hermocopides scandal see, for example, R. Osborne, "The Erection and Mutilation of the Hermai," *Proceedings of the Cambridge Philological Society*, n.s., no. 31 (1985): 47–73. —Trans.

28. See Seneca, *Epistles* 90.14.

29. See Juvenal, *Satires* 14.308.

30. See the translation of Diogenes Laertius 6.23 in M.-O. Goulet-Cazé, ed., *Vies et doctrines des philosophes illustres* (Paris: Le Livre de Poche, 1992), 707n3.

31. See the versions published by Éditions des Belles Lettres of Julian's *Contre les Cyniques ignorants* 20 and *Anthologie palatine* 7.64.

32. See É. Marlière, "Le tonneau en gaule romaine," *Gallia* 58 (2001): 181–201.

33. See Aristophanes, *Knights* 790.

34. See Diogenes Laertius 6.37; also *Gnomologium Vaticanum* 185.

35. Diogenes Laertius 6.35.

36. John of Damascus, *Excerpta ex cod. ms. Florentino Sacrorum* 2.13.87; quoted in Paquet, *Les Cyniques grecs*, 96–97.

37. See Diogenes Laertius 6.22.

38. *Gnomologium Vaticanum* 196.

39. Stobaeus, *Florilegium*, ms. M, 5.67; quoted in Paquet, *Les Cyniques grecs*, 141.

40. Lucian, *Philosophies for Sale* 9, trans. A. M. Harmon (Cambridge, MA: Harvard University Press, 1915).

41. Diogenes Laertius 6.56.

42. Plutarch, *Sayings of Spartans* 56 [= 235e], trans. F. C. Babbitt (Cambridge, MA: Harvard University Press, 1931). [Babbitt's version slightly modified. —Trans.]

43. See Diogenes Laertius 6.49.

44. See Diogenes Laertius 6.73.

45. See Quintus Curtius Rufus, *Histories of Alexander the Great* 3.1, 4.5.8.

46. Schol. Aeschines 2.83.

47. Aelian, *Historical Miscellany* 13.28.

48. Diogenes Laertius 6.55.

49. See Dio Chrysostom, *Discourses* 10.

50. *Gnomologium Vaticanum* 195.

51. See Diogenes Laertius 6.74.

52. Sextus Empiricus, *Against the Professors* 7.53; quoted in J. Brunschwig, "Démocrite et Xéniade," in *Proceedings of the First International Conference on Democritus*, 2 vols. (Xanthi, Greece: International Democritean Foundation, 1984), 1:110.

53. Diogenes Laertius 6.74.

54. Julian, *Orations* 6.15 [= 196a], trans. W. C. Wright (Cambridge, MA: Harvard University Press, 1913).

Chapter 3

1. Galen, *On the Affected Parts* 6.15, trans. M.-O. Goulet-Cazé, in "Le cynisme ancien et la sexualité," *Clio: Histoire, Femmes et Sociétés* 22 (2005): 21.

2. Diogenes Laertius 6.46.

3. Diogenes Laertius 6.69.

4. See Dio Chrysostom, *Discourses* 6.16–20 [= *Diogenes, or On Tyranny*].

5. Diogenes Laertius 6.3.

6. Diogenes Laertius 6.105.

7. See S. Husson, *La République de Diogène: Une cité en quête de la nature* (Paris: Vrin, 2011).

8. Dio Chrysostom, *Discourses* 10.29–30 [= *Diogenes, or On Servants*], trans. J. W. Cohoon (Cambridge, MA: Harvard University Press, 1932). [With regard to cannibalism, Diogenes objected to taboos against the eating of human flesh on naturalistic grounds, drawing upon arguments developed by the pre-Socratics, especially Anaxagoras; see Diogenes Laertius 6.73 and the gloss by R. Hard in *Diogenes the Cynic: Sayings and Anecdotes* (Oxford: Oxford University Press, 2012), 202n215. —Trans.]

9. Theophrastus, *Megarian Dialogue*; quoted in Diogenes Laertius 6.22.

10. See Diogenes Laertius 6.78; *Greek Anthology* 1.285.

11. *Gnomologium Vaticanum* 194. [I have substituted this passage for the more compact formulation found in *GV* 169, cited in the French edition; *Diogenes the Cynic: Sayings and Anecdotes*, trans. Hard, 24–25 (see also 189n88). —Trans.]

12. Dio Chrysostom, *Discourses* 8.11 [= *Diogenes, or On Virtue*]; quoted in Léonce Paquet, *Les Cyniques grecs: Fragments et témoignages*, 2nd ed. (Ottawa: Les Presses de l'Université d'Ottawa, 1988), 197.

13. Diogenes Laertius 6.55.

14. Johannes Stobaeus, *Florilegium*, ms. M, 13.27; quoted in Paquet, *Les Cyniques grecs*, 93.

15. Plato, *Republic* 375e, trans. Chris Emlyn-Jones and William Preddy (Cambridge, MA: Harvard University Press, 2013).

16. Diogenes Laertius 6.60. [Mensch's version slightly modified, following *Diogenes the Cynic*, trans. Hard, 25, no. 89. —Trans.]

17. Diogenes Laertius 6.40. [A veiled rebuke of Plato's own behavior in returning to Sicily; cf. Aelian, *Historical Miscellany* 14.33 and *Diogenes the Cynic*, trans. Hard, 194n130a and 195n130b. —Trans.]

18. Diogenes Laertius 6.46.

19. *Gnomologium Vaticanum* 96; *Diogenes the Cynic*, trans. Hard, 55, no. 241.

20. See, for example, Homer, *Iliad* 1.4–5, 22.66–71, 24.406.

21. See C. Franco, *Shameless: The Canine and the Feminine in Ancient Greece*, rev. ed. (Berkeley: University of California Press, 2014).

22. See T. Dorandi, "Filodemo: *Gli Stoici* (Pherc. 155 E 339)," *Cronache Ercolanesi* 12 (1982): 91–133.

23. Augustine, *City of God* 14.20, trans. Philip Levine (Cambridge, MA: Harvard University Press, 1966).

24. See Diogenes Laertius 6.86.

25. See, for example, Apuleius, *Florida* 14.

26. See *Florilegium Monacense* 156.

27. See Diogenes Laertius 6.88, 6.96–97.

28. Diogenes Laertius 6.96.

29. Fragment quoted by Diogenes Laertius 6.93.

30. See Diogenes Laertius 6.88.

31. Demosthenes, *Orations* 48.53, trans. A. T. Murray (Cambridge, MA: Harvard University Press, 1939).

32. Diogenes Laertius 6.54. [Here I prefer R. D. Hicks's 1925 Loeb rendering to Mensch. —Trans.]

33. Al-Mubashshir ibn Fatik, *Selected Maxims and Aphorisms* 5; quoted by D. Gutas, "Sayings by Diogenes Preserved in Arabic," in R. Goulet and M.-O. Goulet-Cazé, eds., *Le Cynisme ancien et ses prolongements* (Paris: Presses Universitaires de France, 1993), no. 210.1.

34. Diogenes Laertius 6.52.

35. See Diogenes Laertius 6.51.

36. Stobaeus, *Florilegium*, ms. M, 6.52; quoted in Paquet, *Les Cyniques grecs*, 92.

37. Diogenes Laertius 6.59. [Hicks's rendering modified, following the standard French version. —Trans.]

38. Diogenes Laertius 6.53. [Here a line from the *Iliad* (5.40) has been altered, concealing a sexual double entendre; see Mensch's note at 208n85. —Trans.]

39. Diogenes Laertius 6.58.

40. Plato, *Symposium* 183c. [Reproducing the author's revised version. —Trans.]

41. Diogenes Laertius 6.60. [Here again I prefer Hicks's rendering. Diogenes uses the word *akrasia*, signifying a lack of self-restraint, on the part of both prostitutes and their male clients. —Trans.]

42. See Diogenes Laertius 6.61.

43. Plutarch, *Moralia* 5c [= *The Education of Children*], trans. F. C. Babbitt (Cambridge, MA: Harvard University Press, 1927).

44. See, for example, Athenaeus, *Learned Banqueteers* 588e–f [= 13.55], trans. S. D. Olson (Cambridge, MA: Harvard University Press, 2010).

45. Diogenes Laertius 6.65.

46. Athenaeus, *Learned Banqueteers* 565c [= 13.18].

47. See Diogenes Laertius 6.46.

48. See Philo, *Every Good Man Is Free* 18.122, quoting Homer, *Iliad* 24.602–604. [I reproduce here the translation by Robert Fagles (New York: Viking, 1990). —Trans.]

49. Stobaeus, *Florilegium*, ms. M, 29.92; quoted in Paquet, *Les Cyniques grecs*, 95. [Medea convinced the daughters of Pelias to cut their father into pieces and cook him in a pot, having first cut up an old ram and added herbs to make a stew, after which a young ram jumped out of the pot. —Trans.]

50. Antonius and Maximus, *On Improper Women* 609; quoted in Paquet, *Les Cyniques grecs*, 96.

51. *Papyrus Bouriant* no. 1; quoted in Paquet, *Les Cyniques grecs*, 96.

52. See Plutarch, *Moralia* 77e–f [= *How a Man May Become Aware of His Progress in Virtue* 5], trans. Babbitt.

53. Diogenes Laertius 6.40.

54. Antonius and Maximus, *On Sobriety* 302; quoted in Paquet, *Les Cyniques grecs*, 94.

55. See Diogenes Laertius 6.6, 6.13, 6.22.

56. See, for example, Diogenes Laertius 2.36, where Socrates says that he can see Antisthenes's vanity through the tear in his cloak. —Trans.

57. See Diogenes Laertius 6.33.

58. See Diogenes Laertius 6.86.

59. Diogenes Laertius 6.85.

60. Sidonius Apollinaris, *Letters* 9.9.14, trans. W. B. Anderson (Cambridge, MA: Harvard University Press, 1965); emphasis added.

61. See Epictetus, *Discourses* 1.24.8.

62. See Sextus Empiricus, *Outlines of Pyrrhonism* 1.153.

63. Diogenes Laertius 6.59.

64. Diogenes Laertius 6.27.

65. See Aristotle, *Rhetoric* 3.10.7 [= 1411a]. [Aristotle attributes this remark to Diogenes, who may have gotten the idea from Antisthenes. —Trans.]

66. Diogenes Laertius 6.34.

67. Stobaeus 3.4.111; *Diogenes the Cynic*, trans. Hard, 20–21, no. 65.

68. See Diogenes Laertius 6.42.

69. See Diogenes Laertius 6.30.

70. Diogenes Laertius 6.27. [Here I give Hicks's rendering; with regard to "digging and kicking," see *Diogenes the Cynic*, trans. Hard, 188n66. —Trans.]

71. Diogenes Laertius 6.49.

72. See Aelian, *Historical Miscellany* 12.58.

73. Diogenes Laertius 6.70.

74. See Diogenes Laertius 6.81.

75. See Diogenes Laertius 6.39. [Here I follow the standard French version in preference to Mensch. —Trans.]

76. See Diogenes Laertius 6.87.

Chapter 4

1. Diogenes Laertius 6.64.

2. Johannes Stobaeus, *Florilegium*, ms. M, 4.84; quoted in Léonce Paquet, *Les Cyniques grecs: Fragments et témoignages*, 2nd ed. (Ottawa: Les Presses de l'Université d'Ottawa, 1988), 91.

3. See Diogenes Laertius 6.57.

4. Aelian, *Historical Miscellany* 14.33.

5. See Fronto, *Correspondence*, Vat. 190 [= Fronto to Marcus Aurelius as Caesar (143 CE)].

6. See Aelian, *Historical Miscellany* 4.11.

7. See the introduction to M.-O. Goulet-Cazé, ed., *Diogène Laërce: Vies et doctrines des philosophes illustres*, 2nd rev. ed. (Paris: Le Livre de Poche, 1999).

8. Dio Chrysostom, *Discourses* 8.1 [= *Diogenes, or On Virtue*], trans. J. W. Cohoon (Cambridge, MA: Harvard University Press, 1932).

9. Diogenes Laertius 6.21.

10. See Plutarch, *Lycurgus* 30.6.

11. See Diodorus Siculus, *Library of History* 15.76.

12. See Diogenes Laertius 6.18.

13. Diogenes Laertius 6.64.

14. Diogenes Laertius 6.40.

15. On this untranslatable witticism, see *Diogenes the Cynic: Sayings and Anecdotes*, trans. R. Hard (Oxford: Oxford University Press, 2012), 193n119. —Trans.

16. Stobaeus, *Florilegium*, ms. M, 13.43; quoted in Paquet, *Les Cyniques grecs*, 52.

17. See Diogenes Laertius 7.121.

18. See Diogenes Laertius 6.69.

19. See Epictetus, *Discourses* 3.22.

20. Diogenes Laertius 6.32.

21. Diogenes Laertius 6.48.

22. See Diogenes Laertius 6.39.

23. Diogenes Laertius 6.57.

24. See, for example, Diogenes Laertius 6.41.

25. See Diogenes Laertius 6.33.

26. Diogenes Laertius 6.41. [Mensch's solecism corrected. —Trans.]

27. Ibn Hindu, *Diogenes* 32; quoted by D. Gutas, "Sayings by Diogenes Preserved in Arabic," in R. Goulet and M.-O. Goulet-Cazé, eds., *Le Cynisme ancien et ses prolongements* (Paris: Presses Universitaires de France, 1993), no. 271.1.

28. See Diogenes Laertius 6.33.

29. See Demosthenes 21 [= *Against Meidias*].

30. See Diogenes Laertius 6.42.

31. See Luciano Canfora, *Un mestiere pericoloso: La vita quotidiani dei filosofi greci* (Palermo: Sellerio, 2000). [A French edition exists, but no English version has yet been made. —Trans.]

32. See Diogenes Laertius 6.43.

33. See Diogenes Laertius 6.90.

34. Diogenes Laertius 6.34.

35. See Diogenes Laertius 6.80.

36. See Diogenes Laertius 6.17–18.

37. On Monimus, see Diogenes Laertius 6.83; on Onesicritus, 6.84; on Crates, 2.15.

38. See Diogenes Laertius 6.95.

39. See Diogenes Laertius 6.80.

40. See Kurt von Fritz, "Quellenuntersuchungen zu Leben und Philosophie des Diogenes von Sinope," (diss., Munich, 1926), published in *Philologus* suppl. 18, no. 2 (1926).

41. Julian, *Orations* 7, 210d [= *To the Cynic Heracleios*], trans. W. C. Wright (Cambridge, MA: Harvard University Press, 1913).

42. See Diogenes Laertius 6.73.

43. *Gnomologium Vaticanum* 201; quoted in Paquet, *Les Cyniques grecs*, 59.

44. See Lucian, *Philosophies for Sale* 9.

45. See Diogenes Laertius 6.48.

46. Diogenes Laertius 6.24.

47. Homer, *Iliad* 5.889. [Here I reproduce the version by Richmond Lattimore (Chicago: University of Chicago Press, 1951). —Trans.]

48. Diogenes Laertius 6.55, quoting *Phoenician Women* 40. [Mensch's inadvertent mistranslation of the Greek *xene* as "friend" corrected here. —Trans.]

49. Diogenes Laertius 6.68.

50. Diogenes Laertius 6.73.

51. Diogenes Laertius 6.72.

52. Diogenes Laertius 6.50.

53. Diogenes Laertius 6.50.

54. Diogenes Laertius 6.58.

55. Diogenes Laertius 9.51.

56. See Sextus Empiricus, *Against the Professors* 1.52, and Cicero, *On the Nature of the Gods* 1.42.

57. See Sextus Empiricus, *Against the Physicists* 1.54.

58. Diogenes Laertius 6.42.

59. Diogenes Laertius 6.63. [Mensch's version slightly modified. —Trans.]

60. Diogenes Laertius 6.39. Diogenes refers here to the Spartan king and Theban general who clashed at Coroneia in 394 and at Leuctra in 371.

61. Diogenes Laertius 6.24.

62. Diogenes Laertius 6.45.

63. Tertullian, *To the Nations* 2.2.

64. See Diogenes Laertius 6.75–76.

65. Diogenes Laertius 6.36.

66. Plato, *Protagoras* 312d, trans. W. R. M. Lamb (Cambridge, MA: Harvard University Press, 1967).

67. See Dio Chrysostom, *Discourses* 4.

68. See *Diogenes the Cynic*, trans. Hard, 207n236a. —Trans.

69. Plutarch, *Life of Alexander* 14.1–3; *Diogenes the Cynic*, trans. Hard, 54, no. 236d.

70. See Diogenes Laertius 6.93.

71. See Diogenes Laertius 6.94.

72. See, for example, Diodorus Siculus, *Library of History* 17.100–101, and Quintus Curtius Rufus, *History of Alexander* 9.7.16–22.

73. See the account by Demetrius of Magnesia in his book *On Men of the Same Name*, cited in Diogenes Laertius 6.79.

74. See Diogenes Laertius 6.94; Pausanias, *Description of Greece* 2.2.4; Aelian, *Historical Miscellany* 8.14; Jerome, *Against Jovinian* 5.17.

75. See Plutarch, *Moralia* 995c–d [= *On the Eating of Flesh* 1.6]; also *Moralia* 956b [= *On Whether Fire or Water Is More Useful* 2].

76. See Diogenes Laertius 6.34.

77. See Diogenes Laertius 6.77.

78. See Diogenes Laertius 6.77.

79. *Greek Anthology* 7.116; Diogenes Laertius quotes himself at 6.79.

80. See Jerome, *Against Jovinian* 5.17.

81. See Lucien Jerphagnon, "Les mille et une morts des philosophes antiques: Essai de typologie," *Revue Belge de Philologie et Histoire* 59, no. 1 (1981): 17–28.

82. Stobaeus, *Florilegium*, ms. M, 40.8; quoted in Paquet, *Les Cyniques grecs*, 151.

83. The Ilissus was a river that ran through Athens. See Diogenes Laertius 6.79.

84. Cicero, *Tusculan Disputations* 1.43.104; *Diogenes the Cynic*, trans. Hard, 82, no. 397b.

85. See Diogenes Laertius 6.78.

86. See Diogenes Laertius 6.31.

87. See Pausanias, *Description of Greece*, 2.2.4.

88. Antipater, *Greek Anthology* 7.77, trans. A. S. F. Gow and D. L. Page (Cambridge: Cambridge University Press, 1968).

89. Leonidas, *Greek Anthology* 7.67, trans. W. R. Paton (Cambridge, MA: Harvard University Press, 1917). [Paton's version very slightly modified. —Trans.]

90. Honestus, *Greek Anthology* 7.66, trans. Paton.

91. Aelius Theon, *Preliminary Exercises* 5; quoted in Paquet, *Les Cyniques grecs*, 99.

BIBLIOGRAPHY

Avram, A., J. Hind, and G. Tsetskhladze. "Sinope." In M. H. Hansen and T. H. Nielsen, eds., *An Inventory of Archaic and Classical Poleis, 960–963*. Oxford: Oxford University Press, 2004.

Babelon, J. "Diogène et la monnaie." *Demareteion* 1, no. 2 (1935): 63–66.

Babelon, J. "Diogène le Cynique." *Revue Numismatique*, 4th ser., vol. 18 (1914): 14–19.

Baldacchino, A. *Diogène le Cynique: Fragments inédits*. Paris: Éditions Autrement, 2014.

Barat, C. "La ville de Sinope: Réflexions historiques et archéologiques." In D. Kassab Tezgör, ed., *Sinope: Un état de la question après quinze ans de travaux (Actes du Symposium International 7–9 mai 2009)*, 25–64 and 533–636. Leiden: Brill, 2011.

Barat, C. "Sinope et ses relations avec la péninsule anatolienne: Réseaux, échanges des biens et des hommes." In H. Bru, F. Kirbilher, and S. Lebreton, eds., *L'Asie mineure dans l'Antiquité: Échanges, populations et territoires*, 351–375. Rennes: Presses Universitaires de Rennes, 2009.

Dan, A. "Sinope, 'capitale' pontique dans la géographie antique." In H. Bru, F. Kirbilher, and S. Lebreton, eds., *L'Asie mineure dans l'Antiquité: Échanges, populations et territoires*, 67–131. Rennes: Presses Universitaires de Rennes, 2009.

Davieau, N. "Le Corps des philosophes: Traditions biographiques et constructions de la personne du philosophe chez Diogène Laërce." Doctoral thesis, Université Paris 1 Panthéon-Sorbonne, 2015.

Desmond, W. *Cynics*. Berkeley: University of California Press, 2008.

Dorandi, T. "Filodemo: Gli Stoici (PHerc. 155 e 339)." *Cronache Ercolanesi* 12 (1982): 91–133.

Finley, M. I. "Diogène le Cynique." In M. I. Finley, *On a perdu la guerre de Troie*, 97–108. Trans. Jeannie Carlier. Paris: Les Belles Lettres, 1990.

Giannantoni, G. *Socratis et Socraticorum Reliquiae*, vol. 2. Naples: Bibliopolis, 1990.

Goulet, R., ed. *Dictionnaire des philosophes antiques*, 7 vols. Paris: CNRS Éditions, 1994–2018.

Goulet, R., and M.-O. Goulet-Cazé, eds. *Le Cynisme ancien et ses prolongements*. Paris: Presses Universitaires de France, 1993.

Goulet-Cazé, M.-O., ed. *Diogène Laërce: Vies et doctrines des philosophes illustres*. 2nd ed. Paris: Le Livre de Poche, 1999.

Goulet-Cazé, M.-O. *Le Cynisme: Une philosophie antique*. Paris: Le Livre de Poche, 2017.

Goulet-Cazé, M.-O., D. Gutas, and M.-C. Hellmann. "Diogène de Sinope." In R. Goulet, ed., *Dictionnaire des philosophes antiques*, 2:812–823. Paris: CNRS Éditions, 1994.

Gugliermina, I. *Diogène Laërce et le cynisme*. Lille: Presses Universitaires du Septentrion, 2006.

Gutas, D. "Sayings by Diogenes Preserved in Arabic." In R. Goulet and M.-O. Goulet-Cazé, eds., *Le Cynisme ancien et ses prolongements*, 475–518. Paris: Presses Universitaires de France, 1993.

Helmer, É. *Diogène le Cynique*. Paris: Les Belles Lettres, 2017.

Husson, S. *La République de Diogène: Une cité en quête de la nature*. Paris: Vrin, 2011.

Navia, L. E. *Diogenes the Cynic: The War Against the World*. Amherst, NY: Humanity Books, 2005.

Paquet, L., ed. *Les Cyniques grecs: Fragments et témoignages*. Paris: Le Livre de Poche, 1992.

Roubineau, J.-M. "Mendicité, déchéance et indignité sociale dans les cités grecques." *Ktèma* 38 (2013): 15–36.

Roubineau, J.-M. *Les Cités grecques (VIe–IIe siècle av. J.-C.): Essai d'histoire sociale*. Paris: Presses Universitaires de France, 2015.

INDEX

For the benefit of digital users, indexed terms that span two pages (e.g., 52–53) may, on occasion, appear on only one of those pages.
Figures in the gallery are indicated by the figure number followed by *f*